The Art of Table Setting and Flower Arrangement

CAREFREE AND SMART Round glass mat carries decoration beneath of fresh acacia and ivy. Podocarpus, leucothoë, euphorbia, green peppers, artichokes, and ivy are arranged on a raised plate-glass stand. Greens in pottery and tumbler, chartreuse napkin, and gray-green figures with a touch of violet-red add unity and contrast. *Arranger: the author.* (Photo: William Sevecke)

The Art of Table Setting and Flower Arrangement

NEW EXPANDED EDITION

BY SYLVIA HIRSCH

Thomas Y. Crowell Company : New York : Established 1834

With love to my children,

C. J. SAM, BRENDA, AND GEORGE

PREFACE

*F*OR several years my students and colleagues have urged me to put into book form the material I have used in my lectures and classes on flower arrangement and table setting. This book is written in response to their requests. Its purpose is to bring both pleasure and ideas to all women everywhere—the young bride, the seasoned homemaker, and the flower show exhibitor.

I hope to show the young bride, starting a new home, how to avoid many pitfalls. I trust she will discover the answers to the basic questions on how to set a beautiful table. She will find practical suggestions on what table appointments to buy and how to correlate them effectively to enhance everyday dining and to make entertaining a special delight.

The book is also intended to aid the seasoned homemaker who may be weary of using the same appointments in the same way. It should stimulate her with refreshing new ideas on how to spruce up her table at little or no cost.

The flower arranger, too, who enjoys the thrill of creating distinctive table settings for exhibition, where originality and smartness are the keynote to prize-winning compositions, will be guided on how to acquire Blue Ribbons.

In addition to providing the practical and technical angles, it is my desire that this book should serve to stimulate everyone who loves beauty. I hope to spark an alertness in the reader to become conscious of the frequently-taken-for-granted things in nature and in everyday living. Above all, I seek to encourage artistic self-expression through the combined arts of flower arranging and table setting.

Since introducing capsule settings for flower shows in *The Art of Table Setting and Flower Arrangement* I have received numerous requests for an enlargement of the subject. The new edition attempts to do just that.

Three additional chapters, "The New Emphasis," "New Categories in Table Setting Section," and "New Concepts," discuss current allied phases of table setting and flower arrangement. They highlight the importance of freedom of expression in creative art today.

I hope the many questions that have come to me from so many instructors, judges, exhibitors, and hostesses are answered here.

ACKNOWLEDGMENTS

Wᴵᴛʜ the utmost pleasure I thank my many friends and colleagues who have graciously shared with me their knowledge and talents, notably Mae Cronin, Diana Gilbert, Madeline Meier, Lucille Tilles, and those whose artistic and beautiful arrangements are pictured herein, their names being set forth under their arrangements.

I am sincerely grateful to my good friend Elizabeth Edmondson, well-known horticulturist and Garden Club leader, for her encouragement and unflagging enthusiasm, which helped make this book a reality.

I wish to express my especial esteem to Osa Mae Barton, colleague, friend, and forward-thinking Chairman of National Council Flower Show Schools, for her co-operation and judicious counsel.

I am indebted to La Rochelle Florists, Anne's Gift Shop, Haas Linens, Osmond Willie, and George Johnson, all of New Rochelle, and to Georg Jensen, Inc., especially Robert Heid of Georg Jensen, Inc., Marghab Linens, Rosenthal China Corp., Bloch China Corp., Syracuse China Co., George Rallis, Inc., Cecile Bartholomae, Helen Dean, Mae Cronin, Irene Frank, Mady Walter, Frances E. Spratt, and Stig Skoglund for their kindness in making available their fine table appointments and choice plant material, and for their sound advice.

I wish to compliment Mrs. Samuel Leezer, of the Pittsburgh Guild of Flower Arrangers and the Churchill Garden Club, for the original design of the container employed by me in the arrangement on page 91.

Also, to National Council of State Garden Clubs my appreciation for permission to quote from the *Handbook of Flower Shows*.

For their painstaking patience and artistry, I commend my photographers William Allen, Vincent P. Cronin, George J. Hirsch, Richard Knapp, William Sevecke, and David L. Steindler, and to all those who contributed photographs.

No acknowledgment would be complete without high praise to Virginia Hyne, Pauline Gross, and Eleanor Mamorsky for their superb technical assistance in the preparation of the manuscript.

In conclusion, my everlasting gratitude and admiration go to my husband for his constant encouragement, sympathetic understanding, and invaluable advice.

CONTENTS

COLOR PLATES

Part One

Chapter 1

CONTEMPORARY DINING

Dining has long been associated with hospitality. From Biblical times, sharing one's bread has been a sign of friendliness. The meaning is much the same today, but as people have become more civilized the presentation has become as important as the sharing, frequently improving the flavor of the bread itself. Thus a beautiful table can create an atmosphere to make good food taste even better, and can establish a feeling of warmth and hospitality which sets the pace for delightful dining.

The times we live in are fast-moving. We are all busy people. Our daily responsibilities challenge us more than ever. As wives and mothers most of us play many roles. Each is a truly mammoth assignment, since we must be confidante, cook, chauffeur, civic worker, hostess, and career woman all in one. Yet many a devoted homemaker manages incredibly well in providing an oasis of peace and relaxation so necessary for happy family living.

The dining room is the setting. Our imagination and skill are the agents that can transform a simple meal into something special.

Setting an attractive table is one of the most rewarding tasks. How we set it depends upon where we set it, and where we set it depends largely upon our way of life or our style of living.

The Dining Room

Today meals are served not only in what we know as the dining room, but in many other sections in and out of the home. Present-day architects and modern home decorators have converted alcoves, combined living-dining rooms, terraces, patios, breakfast nooks into some of the most pleasant and delightful dining areas.

Where we dine has much to do with the first step in planning our whole setting. Generally any area where meals are served is referred to as the dining room; whether the area is permanent or temporary, formal or informal, traditional or contemporary, large or small, it doesn't matter. The dining room has been known for centuries as the meeting place for family and guests at mealtime.

Today, with the renewed interest in home decoration, the approach to dining and entertaining is simplified and more direct than formerly.

It would be foolhardy to attempt to buy and assemble your table appointments, as did the brides of years ago, without giving thought and consideration to your style of living and the space in which you do your dining. The size of the room, the decorative background, and the accessories are of utmost importance. The size of the area will help you determine the size and shape of your table. Your planned background sets the style for your table and its appointments. Ask yourself if what you have planned reflects a particular period—French Provincial, Georgian, Early American, or Modern. Or do you plan to combine several periods, which, if well blended, give a pleasing contemporary air?

Be cautious about buying your good china, crystal, silver, or linens. First give serious

WARM HOSPITALITY Grays, lavenders, and pinks blend with the background of stone and wood and echo the hues in the chairs. Lavender iris and stock, pink carnations, purple bronze dracaena, galax, and aspidistra cleverly curved make the twin arrangements of usual plant material highly distinctive. Appointments: pearl gray damask doilies; elegant crystal urns, candlesticks, and glassware; white and green china; and pink glass entrée plates. *Arranger: Mrs. Herbert Herrman.* (Photo: William Sevecke)

thought to the spirit and atmosphere of your dining room. You should never lose sight of it in planning your table, because in choosing your background you have already established your mode of living. Consistency is essential.

The Background—Your Guide

The background not only influences the style, but also suggests the colors that would be most compatible and harmonious. The degree of formality also is indicated by the background.

Lighting, too, plays a striking part in the atmosphere of your room and table setting. Various effects are created by different types of lighting. The crystal chandelier produces an intimate glow. Indirect lighting is soft and gentle. Ceiling spotlighting is dramatic and highlights specific areas of the table or room. By far the most enchanting of all light is candlelight, which has an elusive and magic quality.

Dining-room lighting should be subdued or semibright, never glaring. Tempered and well-distributed lighting can do much to flatter faces, spotlight food, add sparkle to crystal, and glamour to the entire setting.

What do we mean by background décor? We mean the walls: are they painted or covered with paper or fabric; are they plain or figured; does the pattern or lack of it reflect a particular period? We also mean the lighting fixtures: are they central, side, or concealed? We mean the furniture, drapes, curtains, pictures, paintings, and other exposed accessories. They all make up the background décor, setting the scene to guide you in selecting your table equipment.

Picture a room with a Wedgwood blue scenic wallpaper, a crystal chandelier, Queen Anne furniture, gold damask drapes and gold rug, a crystal and silver epergne on the table, and a still-life painting or portrait hung over the fireplace. Without a doubt this background décor spells formality and indicates a specific period—Georgian. Obviously, the china, silver, crystal, and linens selected for this room should reflect elegance. For instance, I would select porcelain of simple design, not fussy or overdecorated, and stem crystal that is exquisite and sturdy rather than delicate. The flatware chosen should illustrate the craftsmanship of the period. For greater latitude, without disturbing the spirit of the room or setting, the table covering may be authentic or a newer concept, such as fine gray linen doilies with white embroidery or a gold organdy cloth. Such a setting would be completely satisfying and harmonious.

Visualize another room with painted walls or with geometric or small-flowered wallpaper, with a brass or wrought-iron lighting fixture and maple, pine, cherry, or fruitwood furniture. The other furnishings include café curtains, a hooked rug, and pewter, brass, or copper accessories. This background décor also indicates period influence—Early American or French Provincial. It also expresses informality. For this room I would select pottery or earthenware with charm, simple flatware, heavy glassware (clear or colored), table covering of medium- or heavy-textured fabrics in contrasting or related colors, thus completing the picture.

5

ULTRA CONTEMPORARY Occident and Orient meet happily in this contemporary setting of white, gold, and black. Venetian blackamoors, Japanese porcelain, English crystal, Danish silver, and Swiss linen are eminently compatible on the mirrorlike black lacquered table. The flower arrangement, so simple and strong, unifies the magnificent appointments of diverse origin—wisteria branches painted chalk white, Phalaenopsis orchids, pittosporum, and nephthytis on a Venetian compote. The green grapes proffered by the blackamoors add a note of contrast. *Arranger: the author.* (Photo: William Sevecke)

Ultra-modern décor expresses simplicity, functionalism, and smartness. The rooms are generally bright, frequently with an entire wall of glass or large windows. The furniture is practical and light in feeling: of metal, wood, or rope, either in lightwood finishes or painted in one or more colors, reflecting the Oriental, Near East, Scandinavian, or Greek influences. Many lighting fixtures are concealed. The drapes or curtains are airy and usually transparent, made of new sun-resistant, easily launderable fabrics. The accessories are generally striking in form and color. New and old art objects and paintings are often used. Dining appointments selected for this room should reflect the same spirit. The china should be plain or of restrained design, the shape striking (coupe or free-form). The glassware should be sturdy and crystal clear. The flatware, which may be either silver, Dirilyte, or stainless steel, should be unadorned but sleek and smart in form. The table covering again offers an opportunity for wide variety. Linen, cotton, chintz, rayon, plastic, and nylon are but a few materials available in a range of solids or patterned designs for doilies and tablecloths.

Most of our contemporary homes do not adhere closely to a specific period. They combine cleverly the best of several periods. Strict formality in table setting and in entertaining is the exception rather than the rule. But whatever the degree of formality, your background décor is still the guide for your table appointments. The table you set should be only as formal as the room itself.

Remember, style, period, color, and the degree of formality are fixed elements that constitute your dining background. They should be the first considerations in selecting and buying your essential appointments. Remember, too, that your appointments must be correlated in *color, texture,* and *spirit* to each other and to the dominant spirit of your background for a subtly harmonious table setting.

ANTIQUES IN A CONTEMPORARY SETTING Rare eighteenth-century china (*porcelain de Paris,* 1790) in black, gold, and blue; Baccarat crystal; Belgian linen and lace doilies; and Onslow silver by Jensen blend harmoniously. An eighteenth-century French ormolu and crystal compote charmingly arranged with white roses (Teena), fuchsia, budding spirea, and forget-me-nots re-echo the colors and elegance of the setting. Background: walls, ivory; hangings, ivory and gold silk taffeta; carpet, celadon; table, Louis XVI faded walnut; chairs, Directoire white with celadon upholstery. *Arranger: Mrs. William Loveman.* (Photo: Martin Linsey)

Present Trend in Table Décor

Our present-day interests, needs, and current fashions are all reflected in contemporary table décor. Our relaxed way of thinking today has caused many change￼ in the way we live and certainly in the way we dine. Strict adherence to ancient forms and customs, slavishly followed in the past, are no longer important. Tables are set today with a great deal of freedom and originality. This liberated attitude has come about from both necessity and choice. Statistics show that we are virtually a servantless country, with about one-tenth of one per cent of the families having regular full-time servants.

Since World War II, industry and science have contributed to our liberated attitude by continuing to introduce a vast variety of new appointments and modern conveniences. Art too plays an important part in our new approach and so does travel. We are exposed to so much more today than we ever were before, through radio, television, and direct contact, and we are indeed receptive.

Today the expression "anything goes" is being taken rather literally by some designers and artists. Freedom of expression is necessary and healthy if art is to progress. It must not be bound too tightly by rules. The artist should be free to interpret what he likes as he likes it. Only the laws of nature, the established art principles, and good taste unconsciously direct his translation into his medium.

With our freer approach and more liberal thinking many things that were never thought of as compatible are being combined successfully. For example, today fine traditional patterned china is very happy in the company of modern Swedish crystal, high-color napery, and modern-line silver. This is certainly a departure from the classical setting, which would have combined delicately etched crystal and white damask with that same china.

There are, however, appointments that are diametrically opposed to each other, and when they are used together in certain ways they are disturbing visually, emotionally, and intellectually. That is because they have no basic compatibility either inherently or in the way they are used. In contemporary table settings things of different origin, style, color, and texture can be used together with interest and success only if they have a common denominator. Appointments must have some relationship in color or spirit. However, one must remember in combining and interchanging the essential appointments (dinnerware, linen, glassware, and flatware) that style, color, texture, and quality need not be identical, but that each must be related enough so as to create a feeling of belonging together. In this way the over-all spirit of the setting is maintained.

Generally, extremes do not produce harmony, any more than they do in personalities, *without* some common interest.

The present trend in contemporary American table settings is eclectic. It is an evolution of various cultures and customs that stem from many countries and from many periods, molded to our present attitude and taste. We have taken the charm, graciousness, hospitality, and some of the elegance of the past and are adapting them to today's more

8

streamlined and relaxed approach. Simplicity with a flair—a smart, sophisticated, consciously styled simplicity, with accents of elegance re-echoing the past—is typical of the present trend in table décor.

Colors are bold or subtle. Period accessories and antiques are used with interest in modern settings, while modern or primitive decorative objects are wonderful notes of contrast in a period setting. Distinctive craftsmanship in equipment and execution is notable. And imagination is limitless.

Beauty is paramount: color and design appeal to the eye and satisfy the aesthetic sense.

A NOTE OF NOSTALGIA Delicate colors and textures reflect the French mood of this traditional setting. Background: ivory walls, apricot damask drapes, spruce green rug. Appointments: embroidered ivory sheer linen cloth, gold-banded china, gold-rimmed goblets, and traditional sterling silver. A French compote holds the graceful arrangement of Orange Delight roses, peach jonquils, ivory freesias, snaps, pale yellow-orange daisies, and variegated ivy. *Arranger: Mrs. Vincent Cronin.* (Photo: Vincent Cronin)

Chapter 2

APPOINTMENTS

$\mathcal{T}$HE essential appointments of a table setting are china, crystal, silver, and linen. They are discussed here only as they are related artistically and practically to table décor and flower arrangements. Linens are discussed in Chapter 3. One could elaborate on each—on the way it is manufactured, the varieties of patterns, styles, comparable values, and places of origin—but that is not possible here. However, the over-all picture will be outlined and the outstanding features and differences noted so that you may feel confident, when selecting your dinnerware and setting your table, that your appointments are well co-ordinated and functional.

Dinnerware

Dinnerware, one of the most important essential appointments of a table setting, can be roughly divided into three general classes: china, pottery, and earthenware.

CHINA

China, sometimes known as porcelain, is fine-textured, nonporous, and translucent. The surface is hard and therefore resists chipping and breaking; with average good care it can last for years. China is made of choice refined clays which are fired at such a high temperature that the clay particles meet and fuse to form a completely nonporous product. China has always been made in formal patterns, but today it is available in many smart semiformal designs which can be used for every day.

Traditional patterns are usually found on formal tables. The richly designed floral patterns of our grandmothers' days—Crown Derby, Coalport, Meissen, Sèvres, and Rosenthal, to mention a few—are exquisite and formal in feeling. But in setting a formal table, we need not follow the tradition slavishly. Even on more formal tables we may employ the new designs and color combinations that reflect elegance, smartness, and newness, which are part of the fabric of life today.

China is manufactured in various weights, some delicate, some sturdy. The price range is wide and is determined by fineness, degree of translucency, and, of course, superiority of design.

POTTERY

Pottery is thick and heavy to the touch. It is coarse-textured and opaque. It is made of common clays that are fired or baked at comparatively low temperatures. Because the temperature is not high, the particles do not meet and completely fuse. As a result, the product is porous and will break and chip more easily. Designs are bold and gay, and this ware is used only for casual and informal settings.

SOPHISTICATED BRUNCH WITH A COUNTRY FLAVOR Burnished, handcrafted rooster serves as inspiration for this smart and beautifully balanced buffet. The textures of the blue-green stoneware, with its dull and satin glaze, contrast delightfully with the nubby pinkish-beige table covering and re-echo the texture and colors of the handsome composition. The weather-vane effect is contrived from three pieces of palmetto. The decorative unit includes strelitzia foliage, mahonia nervosa, and echeveria rosettes. *Arranger: Mrs. Edwin Duryea.* (Photo: William Sevecke)

EARTHENWARE

Earthenware is compounded from more selected clays with other ingredients added to give a whiter body. But it is still fired at a relatively low heat, and like pottery it is opaque and porous. It will break or chip less easily than pottery, but more easily than high-fired china.

There is a type of soft ware that is fired at a higher temperature than the others, which is spoken of as fine earthenware or queen's ware. Josiah Wedgwood perfected this fine earthenware in the late 1700's. Queen Charlotte was so delighted with it that she allowed it to be called "queen's ware." In America this product is known as *semi-vitreous china,* as distinguished from genuine china, which is called *vitrified.*

To tell the difference quickly between china and earthenware, hold a plate and strike it sharply upon the edge with a pencil. If it has a bell-like tone, you will know it is china. Earthenware and pottery produce a dull, unmusical tone. Another way to recognize china is to test it for translucency. Hold a plate up to the light; if it is translucent, you will see the silhouette of your hand through the plate.

Whenever it is possible to purchase china, you will find it to be the better investment because of its durability. However, there are certain textures and patterns that are found only in earthenware and pottery. Though they are not as serviceable, you may be willing to forfeit practicability for the charm and effectiveness they will bring to your setting, particularly to Colonial and Provincial settings.

In selecting dinnerware, remember to select not only by pattern but by type of ware as well. Look for a pleasing shape and an attractive design, one of which you will not tire. Your personal taste will be your guide. If you plan to add to your dinnerware later, select a pattern that will continue to be produced for some time (open stock). Be sure it is in keeping with the spirit of your home—traditional, contemporary, or modern.

Good china is like a basic dress. If it is fundamentally right in style, pattern, and color, it can be dressed up or down for more formal and less formal occasions. One good service, matching or thoughtfully assembled, a variety of table covers, correlated accessories, and a smart floral arrangement can bring diversity to your table setting.

Unlike silver, it is not the basic ingredients that determine the cost of china, but rather the artistry and manufacturing techniques involved in production. Whether you prefer gay, simple, or sophisticated china, you should be able to satisfy your own taste in style and pattern at your own price level.

Not too long ago it was a requisite for a young bride to have at least one complete set of china for special occasions. Styles and buying habits have changed. Today few of us buy complete sets of matching china. We are place-setting conscious. Most young brides, after some study and advice, select a pattern and assemble their china by place settings. A place setting generally includes five pieces—dinner plate, bread-and-butter plate, salad plate, and cup and saucer. This is a good way for young or inexperienced homemakers to make their first selection.

More experienced or venturesome hostesses may assemble their dinnerware by courses, with emphasis on varied sets of plates with different designs and patterns. The change in design, color, and pattern adds interest and variety to the dinner table and keeps table setting and dining from becoming monotonous. In assembling a service by courses, be sure to have it harmonize. The bread-and-butter and dinner plates should match.

The service plate, when used, should not be too busy, since it must receive the entrée plate or soup dish or cup. The dessert plates, cups, and saucers may be as colorful as you like. They may match or not, as you choose, but they must be related in type and harmonious in color.

If you select china or porcelain for your service, be sure to use it from first course through dessert. Do not combine pottery or earthenware with fine china; it is as incompatible as walking shoes with a party dress. The same is true of pottery or earthenware—you may vary the patterns and colors as long as there is harmony and the spirit is right.

Assembling china either by courses or place settings provides for variety and flexibility. A new salad, dessert, or entrée plate may be added from time to time. To create a new picture, try crystal, either clear or in a color that plays up a color note in your basic china.

Your dinnerware is one of the most important accoutrements of your table setting. Because its pattern, color, and style appear with each setting, it commands great attention through repetition.

It is generally difficult to replace china because of the cost and the storage space required. So select it with extreme care and thought, with an eye to its flexibility in blending with and complementing the décor of your dining room. If your china is basically right, you will enjoy it every time you use it—and you will be using it for many years.

To summarize, there are a number of things you should remember in selecting dinnerware:

1. *Type:* China, pottery, or earthenware, appropriate for your living: formal, semiformal, or informal.
2. *Shape:* Simple and pleasing—coupe, square, and traditional styles.
3. *Design:* Attractive, but not too busy.
4. *Color (or Colors):* Appealing, versatile, and satisfying; easy to live with.
5. *Open Stock:* In order to be able to add or replace.

Flatware

Every bride, even though she is a new homemaker and generally inexperienced in buying and co-ordinating table equipment, is aware of the importance of selecting her permanent flatware. It is probably one of the first accoutrements of her table that she thinks about, studies, and gets excited about. Whether she favors heirloom silver, a replica of the past, or a modern version, it must be selected with an eye to her future mode of living.

Beautiful sterling silver, lovely plated silver, Dirilyte, or stainless steel offer limitless styles and patterns from which to choose. Whatever the preference, it must be selected with care and a great deal of thought, particularly if it is her only service, as is frequently the case.

13

ENTENTE CORDIALE Vivid colors ar
bright accents spice this gay and inform
cocktail hour. Bittersweet linen cloth, with va
colored round napkins (uniquely folded), is
foil for brass, wood, and crystal appointment
The outline of the flower arrangement echo
in reverse the plumage of the proud brass coc
The colors in the tropicana roses, greens (nigh
blooming cereus, echinops, hosta), and grap
interpret beautifully the color and spirit of th
sparkling buffet. *Arranger: Mrs. William Fran*
(Photo: Vincent Cronin)

STERLING SILVER is luxurious, elegant, and most durable. Do not keep it only for special occasions. By all means use it for every meal, every day. You will find that it looks lovelier, acquires a lustrous patina, when it is put to frequent use.

PLATED SILVER, particularly the old Sheffield, is equally luxurious and charming, although it is not quite as durable or expensive as solid silver.

DIRILYTE can bring a golden glow to your table. Made of a gold-colored metal alloy that is as solid and serviceable as it is beautiful, this flatware is made only in a few simple, sophisticated patterns. The color is warm and bright, yet subtle; the finish is luxurious. It is a perfect complement for handsome gold-edged or gold-trimmed china, crystal, and accessories. It is a charming accent in a more formal contemporary setting.

STAINLESS STEEL is one of the most popular and practical flatwares. It is favored by young homemakers today because it requires little care. There is infinite variety in design and quality, ranging from the inexpensive ware to the more beautifully finished Swedish and Danish flatwares, some of which are as satiny in finish and as high in cost as silver. Today's stainless steel is typically twentieth century. It can be used appropriately for any informal occasion.

Assemble your flatware as you do your china—by place settings. A basic place setting contains five or six pieces (dinner fork, dinner knife, salad or dessert fork, soup spoon, teaspoon, and butter spreader). Luncheon or entrée forks and knives, dessert spoons, bouillon spoons, demitasse spoons, oyster forks, iced-tea spoons, and other pieces may be added later.

Select flatware from the standpoint of beauty, flexibility of use, and quality. Simple designs of limited ornamentation are easier to maintain and are adaptable to most settings. Pleasing proportion and comfort in handling (as to shape and weight) are all-important factors to be considered in selecting your flatware.

14

Glassware

Glassware is another of our essential appointments. Its transparent quality, catching the light, lends a special air of glamour to your table.

It is hard to realize that this clear, bell-like ware is made from grains of sand, magically transformed into crystal. This ancient process has changed but little over the centuries. Although special types of sand are the basic ingredients of glass, other additives give glass the varied appearance characterizing the different kinds. For instance, what is known as *blown glass* is fine, clear, and highly polished, whereas *pressed glass* may not be as clear or fine, and is heavier.

BLOWN GLASS has red lead and potash added to the sand. It is fired at a very high heat to become molten liquid, which when cool is clear and transparent. Blown glass is delicate, thin, brilliant, and hard. It has a musical, bell-like ring when struck. Fine crystal is glass with a high lead content, usually hand-blown. Sometimes, however, it is blown into molds. Crystal is thus glass of superior brilliance, colorless or slightly tinged, although generally thought of as clear.

PRESSED GLASS is most suitable for production of household articles. The smooth sides may not be as pleasing to the eye as the results obtained by cutting, but the method is so much less costly that it enables many people to acquire products of quality which would otherwise be beyond their means.

Table glassware is indeed varied. To know just which type, style, design, or quality is right, we must be aware of the way we intend to dine and entertain. We must also choose glassware that is related in type to our other appointments. These two considerations narrow our field of choice.

Now we are ready to determine the particular glasses we require: water goblets or tumblers; wine, champagne, and parfait glasses; dessert dishes, and finger bowls, as well as salad and under plates.

As we go about selecting our glassware, it is well to know exactly what is meant by type, style, design, and quality of glassware.

TYPE of glassware refers to the purpose for which it is used: water, wine, cocktail, champagne, parfait, and so forth.

STYLE enters our discussion when we speak of stemware, low-footed glasses, and tumblers, for example.

DESIGN refers to shape, contour, proportion, superimposed patterns, bands, and other decorations which may be applied, etched, or cut.

QUALITY has to do with content and craftsmanship. It reflects itself in clarity and texture (bell-like quality), flawlessness, and polish. By considering these qualities we can differentiate among hand-blown, pressed, and cast glassware.

Formal and semiformal settings are associated with crystal, fine tall stemware of simple elegance, luster, and purity, clear or faintly tinged. *Informal settings* suggest tumblers, low-footed goblets of heavier textures, clear or in color.

Colored crystal has become very popular. It adds a dramatic note to your table, emphasizing the pattern in your china, the color in your linens, or in your floral composition. Your crystal should be related in color to one or more of the other accoutrements. The repeated color brings further harmony and co-ordination to your table setting.

Choose glassware that is simple (not ornate or overpatterned) in design, and you will find it not only more adaptable, but always in good taste. Blend it with your china, linen, or floral decoration in color, texture, and spirit, for the most pleasing results.

The proper selection of appointments is sound economy, no matter what the cost. Nothing is expensive if it is right. It is false economy to buy cheap things, poor in quality and style, which have to be replaced frequently. Assemble good appointments gradually. Buy the best you can in design and quality, within your means. Select appointments that are functional, that is, those that serve their purpose well, have more than one use, and are interchangeable. They are more economical in the long run.

Quality pays, so invest in good basic appointments. Fashions change, but good taste is never out of style.

AL FRESCO BUFFET Branches of young elm and Prince of Orange tulips rhythmically repeat the lines of the simulated "bird," composed of embryo palm and yellow and green plastic feathers. Appointments, beautifully co-ordinated, are yellow linen cloth, brown napkins, green Swedish pottery plates and bean pots, orange coffee pot, teakwood salad bowl, and stainless and teak flatware. *Arranger: Mrs. J. L. Webb.* (Photo: Del Van Dusen, *Houston Post*)

Chapter 3

TABLE COVERINGS

THE table covering is an important part of the setting because it occupies such a large area. It serves as background for and should be related to one or more of the appointments in color and texture, but should remain as a background. For example, subtle grayed or pastel colors make effective table covers. Although brilliant or dark colors may be smart for display or outdoors, they are generally difficult to live with. Used for display, their purpose is to attract attention for the moment. The outdoors is so expansive that the sky and nature neutralize some of the intensity of brilliant colors.

When selecting your table coverings, there are several questions you should ask yourself:

1. COLOR. Is it related to the background and appointments? It should be both subtle and beautiful.

2. PATTERN. If woven, appliquéd, or printed, is it interesting and artistic? The pattern should not be too busy.

3. APPROPRIATENESS TO OCCASION. Is it formal, semiformal, or informal?

4. DURABILITY. Is it serviceable? Will it wear well?

5. PRACTICALITY. Can it be washed or must it be cleaned? Brocades, nets, taffetas, chiffons, acetates, and felts are sometimes used for display, but are not practical for home use.

Tablecloths or doilies may be used for either formal or informal occasions. The quality, texture, style, and color differentiate the two. Not too long ago only a cloth, preferably of damask or lace, was considered formal. But today the most exquisite doilies of fine linen and embroidered organdy are designed and used for formal settings. Some of these outstandingly beautiful doilies and tablecloths are on exhibit at the Metropolitan Museum of Art as representative of our twentieth-century styles.

Tablecloths

The cloth should be selected with an eye to the correct size for each table. There is no set rule, but there should be a graceful drop or overhang anywhere from 12 to 18 inches, according to the size and type of table. A cloth that is longer would be uncomfortable for your guests. A shorter cloth would be out of proportion; the table would look like a child in an outgrown dress. The cloth for a buffet table, exhibition, tea, or display table may be a little longer, but for practical purposes it should not touch the floor. (Exceptions: When depicting a Victorian tea table, a fringed cloth to the floor would be in keeping; also at wedding receptions where the table is raised on a dais, or for special tea tables, a full tablecloth skimming the floor is both acceptable and effective.)

Place Mats and Doilies

Doilies are popular because of their variety and ease of laundering.
1. SHAPES. Round, oblong, oval, shell, and others.
2. SIZES. Round doilies should be approximately 15 inches in diameter; others should be approximately 12 by 17 inches.
3. PLACEMENT. May vary from edge of table, depending upon the design. Large round doilies (17 to 18 inches in diameter) may drop off the edge a little. Rectangular doilies should be placed either at the edge or a half inch from the edge of the table. Space between settings should allow for easy, comfortable service, approximately 20 to 24 inches.

SHADES OF LAVENDER AND SILVER Gray satin damask, silver candlesticks, and amethyst crystal blend successfully with either setting. On the left, Theodore Haviland's Arbor, bordered in violet and amethyst, and a crystal goblet; on the right, a silver-banded place plate, Contessa by Flintridge, amethyst crystal plate and stemware. In the values of violet and red-violet, heather, snapdragons, tulips, salpiglossis, and mignonette, camellia and begonia foliage are arranged horizontally. *Arranger: the author.* (Photo: William Sevecke)

Frequently when doilies are used for place setting, the center of the table is left bare. This is particularly interesting if the bare table is attractive. And it is most advisable if the table is narrow, because it gives the table a spacious instead of a choked or crowded appearance.

If your dining table is well-treated, protected against heat, water, or liquor stains, you may reverse the scheme and use only a center runner and no doilies under your china. Tables of marble, glass, or simulated woods (Formica, Micarta, etc.) may also be set in this manner, with no table coverings. They are striking and smart, but belong primarily in a contemporary or modern setting.

Napkins

Today's napkins are varied in form, and some are quite different from those used in the past.

1. FOR FORMAL SETTINGS. The napkins should be the *same* as the cloth, except in the case of lace or organdy. With those fine linen of similar color may be used, and the corner or some other portion of the napkin may repeat the decoration of lace or appliqué.

2. FOR INFORMAL SETTINGS. The napkins may *match, blend,* or *contrast* in color and texture with the table covering.

3. FOR SEMIFORMAL SETTINGS. The napkins may *match* or *blend,* but *never contrast* in color, and rarely in texture with the table covering.

4. SIZES. There have been several changes in the past few years. The large 24-inch napkins of our grandmothers' days are no longer in use. Instead, designers and authoritative sources state that a smaller napkin is more comfortable, in better proportion to the much-favored and approved place mats, and in perfectly good taste for either luncheons or dinners.

Table décor stylists are like the fashion industry designers—they are not in complete accord as to the specifications of napkin sizes. Some stylists favor a conservative approach, some take a more extreme attitude. The most universally accepted sizes today are as follows:

Dinner napkins, approximately 17 to 20 inches

Luncheon napkins, approximately 15 to 17 inches

Tea napkins, approximately 11 to 12 inches

Note. Napkins used with mats or doilies should be approximately 17 inches to be in good proportion. The 17-inch napkin with doilies may be used for either formal or informal occasions.

FOLDING. Because of the many changes in the design of napkins that are constantly taking place, there are no longer rigid rules for folding them. It is logical that with the many shapes presently used (square, rectangular, crescent, round, or oval) there can be no one way to fold a napkin properly. Good taste, neatness, simplicity, and expediency are your only guides. Avoid fancy folds. Keep them as neat as the shape will allow.

For formal dinners a napkin is often folded in thirds and again in thirds, so that the monogram appears in the center; then it is formed into a soft roll by folding back both sides. Another way is to fold the napkin like a book, neatly and with precision.

PLACEMENT. As a necessary accoutrement the napkin should contribute to the balance but should not command undue attention or distract from the over-all design of your table. It should be placed at the left of your setting, about one inch from the edge of the table or in line with the lower edge of the mat.

If folded like a book, either the open edge or the folded edge may face the plate, although practically and artistically it is preferable to place the open edge toward the plate.

For very formal occasions, when the first course is not already on the table, the napkin may be folded simply and exactly and placed in the middle of each service plate.

How to Increase Your Linen Wardrobe

Charming, appropriate table covers within the limits of the average purse can be bought, dyed, or made, depending on the desire and talent of the homemaker.

The ambitious and ingenious person finds it fun to make her own tablecloths, doilies, and runners. A wide choice of practical fabrics are available today. For instance, there are linen, rayon, nylon, cotton, woven fabrics, organdy, horsehair, plastic, and many others. They present an extensive range in colors, textures, and patterns that afford delightful artistic possibilities.

TABLECLOTHS

Tablecloths are easily made. Allow two 36-inch widths for the average table, unless you can find a 72-inch material that you like. The length depends upon the size you wish the finished cloth to be. When two widths are used, use one full width for the center of the table. Cut the other width in half, lengthwise. Seam either side of the full width. If your table is narrow, or if your fabric is wide, you may have to cut the center strip a little narrower. Press seams flat. For a lovely cloth, hand-hem both cloth and napkins. Insertions of lace, embroidery, or appliqués can be added for elegance and individuality.

Doilies and Mats

The horsehair doily pictured is easy to make. Use two-inch and four-inch bands of horsehair that may be purchased in a millinery supply store. There is thread on both edges. Draw the thread carefully on one side until the entire length is shirred to make a closed circle in the center. Fasten securely. Do the same with the next band and attach to the outer edge of the center circle. Have all seams meet at the same point and hand-sew with tiny stitches. Press seams. Repeat until the doily is the desired size—about 17 or 18

SHEER DELIGHT Sea-foam green horsehair doilies lend elegance and style. Something new enhances something old. The antique cut glass compote holds an arrangement of pale pink garden roses, violets, and euonymus. *Arranger: the author.* (Photo: La Crosse, Wisc., *Tribune*)

inches in diameter. The material for this doily costs approximately $2. If purchased ready-made, each doily costs about $20.

Other doilies or place mats of fine- or coarse-textured fabrics can easily be made. Rectangular doilies should be approximately 12 by 17 inches. A variety of other sizes and shapes can be made, however. If you plan a novel shape, make a paper pattern first. Be sure, however, that doilies are not too large for your table or too small to hold your basic setting.

ROUND GLASS MAT

Have a glazier cut a 15- or 16-inch circle of quarter-inch plate glass and bevel the edges smooth. This is a very smart and versatile mat (see page 22). It may be used with any color china. An array of designs can be created under the mat and you can originate different designs for different settings by using fresh, dried, or artificial material. This glass mat is cool, crisp, and smart—a delightful complement for the spring or summer table. It is definitely a laundry saver, but care is needed in storing. Either place felt between the mats and lay them flat, or have a rack built (much like a record or tray rack) into which you can slide them. The cost per mat is about $1.50. Rectangular mats with round edges are also attractive and practical.

ROUND GLASS MAT
Smart and utilitarian.

DYEING AND TINTING

Color is stimulating and plays an important part in our lives today. Old embroidered Italian linens and fine white damasks that you may be tired of can be revived and made attractive by dyeing. Good results can be had by following the directions on the dye box and using your washing machine. For subtle or unusual colors, you can mix two or more dyes. When doing this, be sure to dissolve the dye in a large vessel and test the color before putting it in your washing machine. Try small articles first, like doilies or bridge cloths, then you will know how to handle larger pieces. Do not experiment with a four-yard cloth!

It is not sacrilegious to dye a beautiful white Irish damask cloth, particularly if you have a number of them piled up on the shelves of your closet. Color, subtle or vibrant, will give your table a lift, and you will enjoy using your beautiful cloth more than ever.

For a new look in your table setting, change your table linen. It is by far the simplest and least expensive way to use the same appointments and to attain freshness. Use your china on a peach cloth—you will find it charming; on a blue cloth it will be serene; on an ecru cloth it will appear elegant; on a yellow, bright and gay.

White cloths can be used effectively if contrasting color notes are introduced. For example, try using accents of ruby red, American Beauty, emerald green, or Persian blue.

By increasing your linen wardrobe, you ensure variety and flexibility of your table setting, diversifying your daily presentation. Even with the same china, crystal, and silver you are able to create a whole new picture.

22

Chapter 4

CORRELATION OF APPOINTMENTS

*I*N planning a table, as in any creative work, one must have an idea, an inspiration. A lovely cloth, beautiful china, an unusual accessory, a dramatic or colorful painting hanging in your dining room may serve as that inspiration. In the same way a particular occasion, such as a birthday, anniversary, or holiday can serve as your starting point. Or perhaps a special menu, Chinese, Italian, or Danish, might spur your thinking.

Whatever your inspiration, start from that point. Select and assemble your appointments, the china, crystal, linens, and silver that you have, and relate them in color, texture, and design to create a pleasing atmosphere. For example, do not use a heavy-textured table covering and coarse earthenware of bright or dark colors for an engagement party; nor should you use dainty organdy doilies, fragile china, and pastel colors for an outdoor terrace supper. In either case, the spirit of the occasion would be violated by using the wrong appointments. The spirit of the engagement party would be better interpreted by the use of elegant, fragile, and charming appointments, while sturdier, more casual appointments would be appropriate for an outdoor terrace supper.

Selecting Essential Appointments

Before selecting your essential appointments and before actually setting a table, there are several things you must consider in order to achieve an attractive, well-balanced picture.

1. Decorative background and accessories in the room. The background sets the style for your table, whether you have a definite period room or a combination of traditional and contemporary. The background not only influences the style, but also suggests the colors and degree of formality of your setting.

23

RICHNESS AND GRACE Elegant appointments beautifully co-ordinated: handsome silver compote, candlesticks, and flatware, by Georg Jensen; linens by Marghab; and exquisite stemware. The delicacy of this lavish arrangement is achieved with pastel flowers. Roses, delphiniums, marguerites, verbena, snapdragons, snow-on-the-mountain, and miniature euonymus. *Arranger: the author.* (Photo: William Allen)

2. Colors that harmonize. They should blend or contrast pleasingly with your background colors.

3. Degree of formality. This is defined by the formality of the room itself. The table setting should not be more formal than the room, or vice versa.

4. Size of table. This determines the scale of some appointments, such as candelabra, bowls, platters; decorative composition; and the number of place settings.

5. Placement of table. This allows varied opportunities for the setting, type of service, and floral arrangement. A table placed in front of a picture window, for instance, would require seating on three sides and the floral arrangement set at the back of the table, either centered or to one side, balanced by candles or an accessory. Pairs of arrangements may also be effective.

6. Occasion. This also determines the degree of formality and the spirit within the scope established by the room.

Pleasing Your Family

Color is a forceful element of design. It has a psychological and emotional effect on its observers. Therefore, it is important to select colors for your dining room and table setting that are pleasing to you and your family. A beautifully set table contributes to a happy family and a harmonious home. A smart hostess chooses those colors that cheer her family and enhance and give sparkle to her personality.

Setting a table may be a wearisome task for some—and that is easily understood when we think of three meals a day, 365 days a year!—but those of us who love beauty and feel the urge to create find it is stimulating and rewarding.

There are many new and interesting appointments available today and new ways to combine our old appointments. We have only to challenge our ingenuity to become aware of the variety and charm that can be brought to our tables. Having interesting appointments is not enough; we must know when, where, and how to use them. The principles of design and good taste plus common sense are the key to this know-how (see Chapter 5).

How to Plan Your Table Décor

When setting a table it would be ideal to have all perfectly correlated silver, linen, china, and crystal, but few of us do. A wise hostess, then, must periodically re-evaluate her equipment.

Table appointments are like letters of the alphabet. The same ones can be organized and rearranged in many ways to give different meanings. The opportunity to be original and express yourself is limitless in this field, which co-ordinates the art and science of happy practical living. By interchanging and rearranging the same appointments skill-fully, one can vary the scheme and change the usual everyday scene. This is particularly important to learn and practice when one's appointments are limited.

One new note can change the picture. Bring into play again those wedding or anniversary gifts which once had little or no appeal for you. Perhaps now with your interest in table décor and flower arranging you will see them in a new light. Reconsider all those compotes, bowls, pitchers, tureens, figurines, odd and surplus china, lamp bases, and outmoded linens so carefully packed away for years. These may present new possibilities and thus may inspire a freshly styled and delightful table.

CHINA

As I mentioned earlier, start with your inspiration. It may be beautiful china, for instance. Plain or banded china is very flexible and is relatively easy to use. It is happy on either solid, multicolored, or decorated table coverings. The color of cloth or mats should be selected to dramatize the china, but should remain a subtle background. If multicolored or patterned china is your choice, a little advanced planning is needed for the most successful results. A solid cloth is a foil for multicolored china. To co-ordinate the two, select one of the less dominant colors or a light value of the dominant color from your china for your linens. This will draw your china to your table covering, unifying the two.

Tie in the glassware with either the table covering or a color note in the china. This is most effective. If colored glassware is not available, clear crystal is always acceptable and in good taste—providing texture, design, and quality are in keeping with the other appointments.

LINENS

If you have lovely linens but only one set of china, possibly white with gold band or a solid color modern coupe shape, you can use your linens for diversity. To relieve the monotony of using the same china day in and day out, vary your table covering in color and style to fit the occasion (see Chapter 3). Add a gay dessert dish, a new salad plate, or cup and saucer from time to time, as suggested in Chapter 2. This will introduce a change in design, color, and possibly in texture, revitalizing your linens and giving a fresh-ness to your whole setting.

25

DECORATIVE UNIT

The decorative unit may be flowers, fruit, vegetables, foliage, or any combination of plants or cut plant material with or without accessories (figurines, candles, compotes, etc.). It should have a definite affinity to either the china, linen, or glassware in color, texture, and spirit.

It is not necessary to repeat in your decorative composition all the colors in your appointments. Frequently, this practice tends to destroy the unity of the table. However, the very experienced can disprove this rule and can produce a truly artistic union. A successful practice is to select one color and its values, allowing it to dominate. If a second or third color is desired, use it in smaller quantities for accent and variety.

ACCESSORIES

Accessories, too, must be consistent in their relationship to essential appointments and the decorative unit. Delicate china and sheer linens are not compatible with terra cotta pottery figurines. Nor should you use an exquisite crystal and silver epergne on a boldly striped, textured cloth.

The same thought that you give to assembling your appointments (china, crystal, silver, and linen) must be applied to accessories. The purpose of their presence is to contribute to, not to detract from, the design and spirit of the table. If your accessories are appropriate in size, texture, color, and mood, then they serve to accent and enhance your nicely organized, established setting.

Express Yourself

Expressing yourself is merely a way of doing or saying what you feel. It is your response to emotional, physical, or intellectual contacts. Do you really do the things you want to do? Or do you do what you think is "the thing to do"? Do your table, your home, your art, your clothes reflect you, or are you and they identical replicas of the current mode?

CAPTIVATING AND GAY Amusing Scandinavian pottery candle holders, predominantly gray-blue, set the theme for this table. Gray-blue woven mats; royal blue goblets; napkins flippantly folded; and gray, blue, and green pottery are set on a Danish teakwood table. White and green striped liriope, Burfordii holly, light and dark blue hydrangeas, chartreuse succulents, and ivy leaves in a teakwood container add to the gaiety. *Arranger: the author.* (Photo: William Allen)

GOOD JUDGMENT Strawberries, apples, lady apples, grapes, and ivy are artistically organized on a brass scale. The table is antique pine. Place mats are aqua *ombré* cotton and plastic. The high-glaze pottery plate is Persian blue and the low-footed tumbler is clear crystal. *Arranger: the author.* (Photo: David L. Steindler)

If you must imitate in every detail the thoughts and styles of others, you are not truly expressing *yourself*. But when you respond with a definite reaction to certain fashions, colors, music, or art, then you have been stimulated. Then your own likes and feelings will flow into what you do and translate themselves into what you say, thus reflecting you.

Table setting, like flower arranging, is just another form of artistic expression. Like your home and your dress, it should reflect your personal taste. Do not be afraid to express your feeling for design and your love of color on your table. Like other creative arts, table décor should mirror your personality and your feeling for style, by putting together things and colors that are typically you. Some of us are courageous and naturally uninhibited. We are eager to experiment with new ideas. Others are more timid and conservative, hesitating to try anything new or express what we feel by introducing anything unorthodox—even to the slightest change in color scheme.

The manner in which we express ourselves varies with our personality and knowledge. But when we understand the basic principles of the art of table setting and flower arrangement and master the techniques, timidity gives way to confidence. Our personal responses plus artistic know-how enable us to express ourselves. If our first attempts appear stilted, constant doing will give us courage, and the fetters of conventionality will soon loosen, allowing self-expression gradually to emerge.

If you like vibrant colors, daring combinations, and casual informality, use them by all means. There is nothing more charming than textured fabrics, polished cottons, chintzes, or ginghams, in stripes, plaids, or checks of gay colors to brighten your setting.

Perhaps you prefer more subdued colors, subtle harmonies, and more conventional designs associated with formality. If you do, follow your leaning. A pastel cloth of damask, linen, or lace, simple-banded china, and fine crystal are equally effective and might more nearly typify and express you.

Do you like old things—antiques or old hand-me-downs, those that were originally good in design? Use them with new appointments. Blend them in color and spirit, and you will have a setting that is individual, delightfully unique. If you prefer

27

homespun, pottery, stainless steel, earthy colors, and a simple arrangement of vegetables and fruit, do not hesitate to say so by using them. Or perhaps you fancy the elegance and daintiness of porcelain, hand-blown crystal, satiny sterling, and delicate, fine-textured flowers—all blended in the glow of candlelight.

Classical appointments used in the traditional manner might be foreign to the person who finds Picasso, Shostakovich, and Calder exciting. But modern appointments, novel ideas in placement and service, unusual color schemes, and plant material in an original presentation may better depict the creativeness of this individual.

The unconventional use of a colorful tureen for stew, mugs for coffee, old-fashioned bone dishes for salad, finger bowls for ice cream, or a vegetable dish for your flower arrangement show a departure from the usual. They reflect your personal preference and so express you.

Whether you design your table in a manner smartly simple, traditionally elegant, functionally modern, gaily casual, avant-garde, or just ultra you, your personal flair and good taste should be emphasized. Whatever you do, try to be original in at least some phase of your décor or setting. If you are, your table will be as fresh as a spring rain or as colorful as an autumn sunset.

But always remember this. No matter what colors, designs, or appointments you select, no matter how formal or informal a setting you plan, the spirit of gracious hospitality must prevail. For without this warm feeling of hospitality your table (often called a "board" years ago), is just a place upon which to set food, thus missing the cordial friendliness that we traditionally associate with dining.

SO COOL AND ELEGANT Black, white, and green set the note for this scheme. White linen and organdy doilies, Lalique crystal, Script china by Rosenthal blend beautifully with pandanus, nephthytis, and snow white coral which surrounds a white candle elevated on a black glass plaque. *Arranger: the author.* (Photo: William Sevecke)

Good Taste

When we say a person has good taste, we mean that he or she has the capacity to discern and appreciate whatever is beautiful, excellent, and appropriate. Such persons are aware of fitness, order, and congruity in all things. When we say that something is in good taste, we mean that it shows discrimination and judgment and reflects in manner and style an aesthetic quality.

Good taste is a somewhat intangible attribute. It may be innate or it may be acquired by association with culture. It is the ability to do, unconsciously, the right thing, at the right time, in the right way. A well-developed sense of taste is never set or arbitrary, but always flexible, taking into account the times, the needs, the interests, and background of the person expressing it.

Good taste is not a fixed quality. What may have been the height of good taste to one generation may be anathema to another. For example, the tango was once considered risqué, and women who smoked in public and wore makeup were looked upon with scorn. Such things were regarded as bad taste in those days, but are now accepted, when performed with propriety, as the essence of good taste.

In the field of table setting, good taste is the application of the principles of design, where beauty as well as functionalism is a consideration.

Good taste today is a preference for simplicity and restraint and an antipathy for the trite and commonplace. It is the balance wheel that tells us how far to go when injecting excitement, drama, sparkle, even humor, into our designs and our living. It is the discerning quality that keeps us from overstepping that narrow borderline between what is attractive and acceptable and that which is garish and vulgar.

Taste is conditioned by habit, age, experience, and geography. Good taste in any place or any period avoids overstatement.

Keys to Successful Correlation

1. *Inspiration.* An idea to express, which may spring from the appointments, accessories, menu, plant material, guest of honor, and so forth.

2. *Imagination.* Courage to be original and ability to visualize the finished whole.

3. *Knowledge.* Skill to select and organize the table equipment and decorative unit and relate them to each other and to background.

4. *Good taste.* A degree of restraint is the mark of the cultivated individual. Good taste gives unconscious direction to creative efforts and aids in achieving beauty.

To repeat, having interesting appointments is not enough. We must know when, how, and where to use them. The principles of design are the key to this knowledge (see Chapters 5 and 6). Add a soupçon of spice and imagination to your selection and execution—the result: a correlated table setting of beauty, smartness, and distinction.

Chapter 5

DESIGN

Good order is the foundation of all good things. EDMUND BURKE

$\mathcal{D}$ESIGNING a table means organizing and co-ordinating colors, textures, and spirit in all the equipment used, in order to say something. The result should be an atmosphere of charm and gracious hospitality. A table that produces an atmosphere has a personality. Be sure, however, that it is positive, not negative, and pleasant rather than unpleasant or indifferent. Pallid colors and weak designs are negative. Discordant colors, unrelated appointments, poor design, or a lack of fastidiousness are unattractive. The atmosphere you wish to create may easily be achieved when thought is given to developing your inspiration, your idea.

SPRING SUNSET The arrangement of pussy willows, anthurium foliage, ti leaves, philodendron, Picardy to tangerine gladioli, and grapes is exquisitely styled. *Arranger: the author.* (Photo: William Sevecke)

DESIGN

An idea is a mental picture of something desired, planned, or proposed. It can best be executed by employing the principles of design, the function of which is to give expression and understanding to that idea.

Design is the conception, evolution, and development of an idea. It is a plan, an intent. It is the organization of many things related and unrelated that, when properly arranged, presents a unified, harmonious whole. Design is the careful selecting and arranging of materials to achieve two aims: *order* and *beauty*.

The principles of design are universal; they are important to the success of all art expressions. Knowledge and understanding of these principles are essential in constructing good design, whether in painting, architecture, music, flower arranging, or table setting.

Terminology of or emphasis on certain principles may vary in different mediums. However, the following principles of design are fundamental to all artistic expression.

Basic Principles

The basic principles of design are *proportion, scale, balance, rhythm, dominance,* and *contrast.*

These principles, when you understand them and apply them practically, help express your idea. Disregard for any of the above in planning your table or any composition may cause one or more of the following: poor equilibrium, busyness, or blatant or discordant color combinations—thus producing disunity, confusion, and unrest.

A table set without regard to principles of design in its organization might well have a personality, but the chances are that it would be one of disorganization and unpleasantness, something which should always be avoided.

Arranging a table is an art. Fashions change through the years, but history has proved that good design in art, as well as in furnishings, has an enduring quality and will outlive transient modes. So choose well. For economy as well as beauty, it is of the greatest importance that every individual understand and appreciate the principles of design. Briefly then, let us review the well-established principles of design and relate them to table décor.

Principles of Design Related to Table Décor

Proportion is the graceful relationship of one part of a structure or composition to another and to the whole. It is sometimes called the law of space relationships. It is closely related to scale, and frequently we find an overlapping. Generally, proportion has to do with height, width, and length. It is form with a harmonious relationship of parts leading to fitness and harmony.

When considering the element of proportion in table décor, there are a number of questions you should ask yourself:

31

STRUCTURAL BEAUTY Dramatic voids contribute greatly to the artistry of this design of garden roses (Talisman buds to blossoms) with bronze rose foliage in crystal. *Arranger: the author.* (Photo: Michael G. Spoto)

Is your tablecloth the proper size for the table—not too long, nor too short? For a seated meal, an overhang of approximately 12 to 15 inches, and for a buffet or tea table, an overhang of approximately 18 inches are in good proportion (see Chapter 3).

Is your flower arrangement or artistic composition comfortably related to its container? Approximately one-and-a-half to two times the height of a tall container or the width of a low container is a pleasing relationship. Generally, arrangements for seated dinners should not exceed 18 inches in height; lower arrangements are preferable.

Is the decorative composition in good proportion to the size of the table? Not so small as to be lost in the center of a large table, nor so large as to be overpowering or inconvenient, thus interfering with the appointments and service. For the average six-foot table, the centerpiece should be 20 to 24 inches in length, or approximately one-third the length of the table.

Scale is the size relationship of component parts that make a specific whole. It is the size relationship of all the elements (containers, accessories, individual blossoms, leaves, and so forth) which make a unit consistent and pleasing. It is the measured relationship of the objects to each other and to the whole so that each assumes its true size.

Scale generally refers to the decorative composition and accessories. For example, very tall, important-looking five-branch candelabra on a 72-inch table would be out of scale; or two small single candlesticks on a 108- or 144-inch table would be inconsistent and out of scale.

32

A large, impressive silver and crystal epergne is out of scale when used as a center-piece on a small table. The beauty of the epergne is lost, since it lacks a proper and adequate setting. The small table appears smaller than it really is, and the large epergne consequently appears overpowering in contrast. A large table is necessary to do justice to such an elegant, imposing centerpiece and to present it in true scale. It is equally inconsistent to use a small arrangement or centerpiece on a large table.

Plant material within the decorative composition must also have a pleasing, consistent relationship. For instance, do not use sweet peas or other small flowers with large chrysanthemums unless they are grouped to make a unit that will appear related in scale. Figurines or accessories must give a feeling of belonging not only in spirit but in scale.

Napkins, too, must be considered. If extremes are used, they will appear out of scale. For example, 20- or 22-inch napkins for luncheon with luncheon plates are incorrect, as are 12-inch napkins for a formal dinner. Both are incongruous because they are unrelated in scale and are therefore inappropriate.

Balance is the equal distribution of weight on either side of an axis, giving a composition the feeling of equilibrium, stability, and repose.

Balance is particularly important to all table settings, and especially in setting buffet tables. You should ask yourself: Are your appointments so placed that a sense of balance is achieved?

PRESENT TEMPO A well-ordered expression of today; a sophisticated organization of plant material, pandanus, sansevieria, ti, and large philodendron leaves is used with obake anthurium on a walnut burl with interest and stability. *Arranger: the author.* (Photo: William Sevecke)

We must remember in this connection that visual weight and actual weight are not the same. Visual weight is a matter of how much attention an object attracts, not how much it actually weighs. For instance, a large object demands more attention than a small one. Also, an object of unusual form or shape is more forceful than one of plain or simple lines. Colors, too, have visual weight. Thus it is that bright or dark colors are more compelling; they are visually weightier than the grays or lighter values.

One way of making sure that a table is in good balance is to divide it mentally into parts or sections. An oval or oblong table should be divided by imaginary lines drawn the length and width of the table. For a round table the diameter would be the imaginary axis. Having determined the sections or divisions (which may be three, four, six, or any division you wish), you should set the table with care. Make sure that each section visually balances each other section. When identical forms, spaces, and colors are used in each section or are in direct relation to the axis, then you have created a *formal* or *symmetrical balance*.

Formal or symmetrical balance is generally (though not always) observed for a seated dinner. It is almost always used for one that is formal, as the name implies.

In *asymmetrical balance,* forms, spaces, and colors need not be identical. A group of small objects may balance a large object. A quantity of grayed or light color can equalize a small amount of strong bright color (see Chapter 6).

Balance may be either symmetrical or asymmetrical, as long as the placement of all appointments creates a pleasing, restful impression.

To achieve balance and equilibrium when you are planning a seated dinner, be sure that all appointments are placed with care and precision, in accordance with the following rules:

1. Placement of mats or doilies: at edge or one-half inch from edge of table (exception: large, round doilies, which may hang over a little, depending on size and style).

2. Distance of silver and china from edge of table: approximately one inch.

3. Proper placement and spacing of utensils within each setting, repeated identically at each setting.

4. Equal spacing between settings.

5. Centerpiece, candles, and accessories should be placed with relation to the center space and the place settings. Small appointments (salts, peppers, ash trays, etc.) should be grouped; they may be placed above each setting, between settings, or distributed to create equal attention.

Symmetrical table settings are generally quiet and dignified; sometimes they are static. Asymmetrically balanced tables, on the other hand, are generally more dynamic. The informal distribution permits flexibility and greater freedom.

Rhythm is related movement, a connected path along which the eye travels easily from line to line, from object to object, from color to color, and from large to small. It unifies the elements by creating a feeling of motion. That motion carries the eye through the design.

34

RHYTHMIC SIMPLICITY   Graceful branches of cocculus create an emphatic rhythmical silhouette. The sensitive placement of coral tulips emphasizes the magnificence of the Kathe Urbach figurine in muted tones of green and peach. *Arranger: the author.* (Photo: Vincent Cronin)

DISCIPLINED NEATNESS
The modified Hogarth curve is drawn with pussy willows. The composition in a Chinese green-bronze vase is a classic demonstration of good scale, proportion, balance, rhythm, dominance, contrast, and harmony: pussy willows, pothos, Picardy and Valeria gladioli (peach to orange-red). *Arranger: the author.* (Photo: George J. Hirsch)

Graceful, measured movement is created through *repetition* and *transition*. Repetition is the use of the same element more than once. Transition is the relative change in *size* from large to small; the gradation in *color* from light to dark, from dull to bright, and from color to color; and in *texture* from rough to smooth, or coarse to fine.

Rhythm in table setting is established when the same appointments, alike in size, form, color, and height, are used within each setting in measured placement. In other words, (1) the china, crystal, silver, and linen must be placed precisely within the designated space on the tablecloth, bare table, or place mat; (2) the spaces between each setting must be uniform; and (3) small objects should be grouped, and groups should be repeated to continue the flow of motion through repetition and transition.

36

Easy transition is produced (1) when groupings of small objects (salts, peppers, cigarette holders, ash trays, nut dishes, etc.) are satisfactorily placed to give visual continuity; (2) when colors are harmoniously related; and (3) when variations in height (from the flat plane of the china and silver to the taller glassware, candles, and flower arrangement) are given consideration. Transition then guides the eye gently around the table, aiding the over-all rhythmic pattern.

Dominance and *contrast* are interdependent. Dominance is emphasis. It consists in presenting one outstanding structural feature to which all else is subordinate. *Note:* Color and texture are considered structural because they cannot be perceived without form. Dominance calls attention to the most important feature by subordinating the less important ones. Contrast is present when we place elements together to emphasize their differences.

Generally speaking, the background of your table should be less conspicuous than the objects seen upon it. Therefore the tablecloth should be one that does not attract too much attention. It should be muted in color and not overly decorated. For exhibitions, special occasions, and outdoor settings, however, striking designs, dramatic colors, or unusual harmonies are acceptable and make effective table coverings.

Dominance can be achieved (1) by choice of unusual shapes, sizes, forms, or colors; (2) by repetition of appointments, colors, or accessories; (3) by placement of centerpiece and accessories; and (4) by contrast of colors or color values. To illustrate: If you use all round forms, all spiky forms, groups of all dark colors or only light ones, you tend to destroy the emphasis by too much sameness. Your setting becomes monotonous. By introducing a slight contrast, you bring the décor into focus; the unification of opposing elements produces a dominant or unified quality.

It is important to remember that contrast to be effective must be limited. It may either be a striking accent, or it may gently point up a dominant feature by relieving the monotony of repetition. As soon as contrast becomes too important or too demanding, it destroys the dominant quality and unity by equalizing attention, and therefore it no longer serves its purpose. Contrast is the necessary spice that adds variety and interest to dominance.

When the aforementioned principles of design are observed, they blend together and the result is unity and harmony. Harmony is the effect of oneness or of blending together.

Knowing the fundamental principles underlying your medium and becoming versed in them gives you, the designer, a sense of support. Understanding them and applying them gives you, the artist, security, freedom, and latitude. Freedom and control are the complements which produce a work of art.

The principles of design are not rigid laws. They are only a guide, a flexible guide, to aid you in artistic self-expression.

Chapter 6

TEXTURE AND COLOR

Texture

TEXTURAL relationship contributes much to a logical and harmonious effect. Texture is the quality by which we differentiate coarse, rough objects from fine, thin, smooth or silky ones. It is a surface finish. It applies to plant material just as it does to fabric, china, crystal, and silver.

In table setting it is simple to blend the proper textures because even the untrained eye can distinguish easily between coarse pottery and fine china, between heavy pressed glass and thin blown lead glass, and between a rough weave and a fine, smooth one. You need only consider the following to make the right selection: (1) style or period of the dining room; (2) its formality; and (3) the spirit of the occasion.

Lovely china, fragile crystal, exquisite linens or lace, sterling silver, a centerpiece of roses, gardenias, freesia, stock, snapdragons, ranunculuses, or other texturally fine flowers arranged in silver, crystal, or porcelain are all hallmarks of the formal setting. These fine appointments are related in texture and spirit; they tell a story of elegance and formality.

Pottery, earthenware, heavy glassware, pewter, homespun or coarse fabric, straw, plastics, and stainless steel spell informality. A decorative unit of vegetables and fruit, squash, pineapple, artichokes or okra with pottery, wood, or metal, texturally says the same thing. An informal setting of this kind would be most appropriate for a casual dining room, outdoor terrace, or game room.

As there are degrees of formality and informality, so there is a wide range of textures, from heavy coarse at one end of the scale to the filmy, delicate, lacy types at the other. The extremes are easy to understand. Most of us would know immediately that a pottery plate on an organdy or Alençon lace tablecloth would be as texturally incompatible as a chiffon dress would be to golf shoes. But the difficulty arises when we move nearer the center of the scale, where the textures are neither very coarse

38

CONTRAST AND SYMMETRY Piquant contrast in colors—pale green linen, dark green crystal and ivy, vivid red anemones and candleholders are smartly accented by the black in the candelabrum, containers, and anemone centers. Twin arrangements and meticulous placement of appointments create a graceful symmetry. *Arranger: Mrs. Walter E. Morse.* (Photo: William Sevecke)

nor very fine, but in-between, such as earthenware or queen's ware (Wedgwood or Spode) and silver plate or stainless steel. These in-between textures may be used to designate a tendency toward either formality or informality. The end result would depend upon the combination of all the appointments, so that the over-all effect is logically harmonious and in keeping with both the dining room and the occasion.

Though textural relationships contribute to the over-all unity of a table setting, one need not be too literal or too exacting. A slight deviation in texture or relative value of appointments is permissible as long as the mood is retained.

Textures have their own distinctive personalities. Like colors, textures communicate specific qualities and convey their own associations. Earthenware, homespun, heavy cottons and linens, and pressed glass seem to say informality and serviceability. Porcelain, damasks, fine laces, and fine crystal create an air of elegance and formality.

The many combinations of fiber fabrics, both natural and man-made, offer endless variations in texture.

Textures are affected by light; dull, uneven surfaces absorb light, while smooth, shiny surfaces reflect light. It is wise to apply the principle of dominance and contrast in selecting your table appointments in regard to texture, for variety and interest. Overdoing or accenting one texture will create dominance, but dominance without some contrast causes monotony and reduces interest. As you can see, to use an over-abundance of silver—flatware, service plates, candelabra, salts and peppers, compotes, nut dishes, cigarette dishes, and so forth—would create dominance, but the lack of diversity also causes monotony. A variety in textures certainly would improve this setting and would enhance the specific appointments.

BURNISHED BEAUTY Burnt yellow, persimmon, orange, and brown—all earthy, warm colors—enliven this buffet. Trim brass appointments, a brown textured cloth, walnut salad bowl, sculptured wood, Royal Copenhagen earthenware (beige, rust, and brown), and deep coral dessert plates are cleverly co-ordinated in texture, color, and design. Podocarpus, coral gladioli, tangerine carnations, Orange Delight roses, ti leaves, and large philodendron, further emphasize color and texture correlation. *Arranger: the author.* (Photo: William Sevecke)

Color

Color is an exciting and forceful medium. It is the keynote to our twentieth-century living. Its role in our lives today can scarcely be exaggerated. We are all color conscious. Everywhere we turn we see color—in nature, in art, in fashion, in our homes, in magazines, and in shops. Our paths are strewn with colors—bold, gentle, dull, or bright—some demanding our attention, others reflecting quietude.

Color is dramatic, stimulating, and provocative. It is the spice of life, but like spice it must be used with discretion and intelligence in order to achieve the height of subtlety and good taste.

The study of color opens new worlds for use and pleasure. It increases our appreciation and understanding of art and nature; it adds considerable glow to everyday living. Can you imagine life without it? It would be dull indeed—gray, neutral, monotone.

Color is many things. It is a science. It causes a physical reaction, an emotional response. Color is that visual sensation that is distinct from form. It is the strongest single influence in our lives, because visual impressions are more intense than those received through any of our other senses.

PATIO LUNCHEON   Gay and beautifully co-ordinated for informal dining are the appointments and the centerpiece. Green grapes, lady apples, limes, peppers, tiny green bananas, geraniums, corn flowers, Scotch broom, and geranium leaves are skillfully arranged in sculptured wood. *Arranger: the author.* (Photo: William Sevecke)

ROSES AND LACE Handmade green linen and white lace doily, green linen napkin, green goblet, etched silver candlesticks, celadon tapers, and green-banded china add to the stately beauty. The arrangement, in a makeshift compote (old silver base and green finger bowl), echoes the lace motif with snow-on-the-mountain and garden roses. *Arranger: the author.* (Photo: William Allen)

Color is reflected light. It results from the play of light waves upon surfaces which reject or absorb certain rays, thus producing the various colors. These light waves, of varying lengths, strike the retina of the eye, and the light waves are then transmitted to the brain through the nervous system associated with the retina. As a result we see what we know as color.

The subject of color is vast. To suggest that it could be adequately covered in this limited space would indeed be presumptuous. My purpose is to introduce the theory and practice of color to you and to acquaint you with enough to whet your appetite so that you may wish to delve further into this fascinating subject. The theory and practice of color will be discussed here only in capsule form, as they relate to the art of table setting and flower arrangements.

SPECTRUM COLORS

Colors the human eye can perceive are called *spectrum* or *prismatic colors*. They are the colors seen in the rainbow. They are also the colors seen when a ray of direct sunlight is allowed to pass through a prism onto a piece of white paper, casting a multicolored band known as the solar spectrum or spectrum band. Spectrum colors are known as *prismatic colors* and are colors of light. They flow and blend into one another, making it difficult to tell where one ends and another begins.

If it were possible to bend the spectrum band into a circle so that the ends would meet, we would have what we recognize as a color wheel. But since this is not realistic, a color wheel has been scientifically devised, the colors of which do not flow together as in the rainbow, but are separated distinctly. Much of the study of colors, their dimensions, and their relations to each other is based upon the color wheel. Therefore, a color wheel will prove helpful in understanding the theory of color more easily.

Eighteen-color wheel
showing sequences of colors.

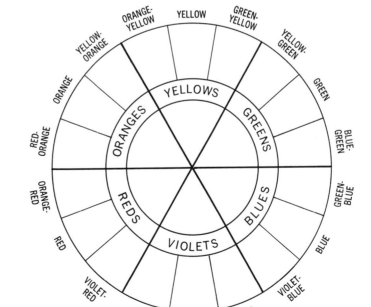

Most authorities agree that six basic colors emerge from the spectrum. They are *red, orange, yellow, green, blue,* and *violet.* The spectrum colors are pure colors of full intensity, not diluted or grayed.

PIGMENT COLORS

The spectrum colors, the colors of light, have been reduced and translated for us by scientists and chemists into tangible *pigment colors,* colors of substance. Pigment colors are surface colors. They are made of animal, vegetable, or mineral matter. We meet these colors in everyday life. They are the colors we work with. An understanding of what they are and what they can do should be most helpful to us because:

1. Pigment color is present in plant material.

2. Most color wheels, particularly the one recommended by the National Council of State Garden Clubs, are based upon the pigment theory with its three color primaries.

3. The pigment theory is used in the mixing of paints and the making of dyes. Therefore, we find a knowledge of this theory to be useful in decorating our homes, planning our tables, and staging our flower shows and exhibits.

PIGMENTARY THEORY

The spectrum colors have been reduced to three basic primary colors: *red, yellow,* and *blue,* from which all other colors can be made by various mixtures, additions, and dilutions.

By mixing a primary color in equal parts with another primary color, we produce a *secondary* color, as follows:

$$\text{Yellow} + \text{Blue} = \text{Green}$$
$$\text{Blue} + \text{Red} = \text{Violet}$$
$$\text{Red} + \text{Yellow} = \text{Orange}$$

If we continue to mix the primary colors with their adjacent secondary colors, we produce the *tertiary* or third division of color.

$$\text{Yellow} + \text{Green} = \text{Yellow-Green}$$
$$\text{Blue} + \text{Green} = \text{Blue-Green}$$
$$\text{Red} + \text{Orange} = \text{Red-Orange}$$

From here on the variations are limitless because of the endless combinations and admixtures which are possible.

THE DIMENSIONS OF COLOR

All colors have three distinct dimensions or qualities: *hue, value,* and *chroma.*

42

HUE

Hue and *color* are synonymous. Hue is the quality by which one color family is distinguished from another: red from yellow; green from blue; red-orange from orange or red. Certain bright hues, such as red and yellow, can be extended further than the blues.

VALUE

Value refers to the lightness or darkness of a color (modulation). The quality by which we distinguish a light color from a dark color is another way of describing value. Values are often called *tints* and *shades,* with certain specific differences in accordance with the amount of white or black which has been added to a basic hue. Thus:

Tint is a light value. White added to a basic hue produces a tint.

Shade is a dark value. Black added to a basic hue produces a shade.

MUTED TONES A composition of low and middle values of violet and green finds counterpoint in a variety of textures and forms for complete harmony. Kalanchoë, echeveria, and begonia foliage are designed around a Pompeian green statuette, by Fred Press, on a matte-finish, gray-green free-form plaque. *Arranger: the author.* (Photo: William Allen)

CHROMA

Chroma is the intensity, purity, or fullness of a color. It is the quality by which we distinguish a strong color from a weak one. It is the strength of a distinctive hue. Chroma is the distance of a color from gray. It is a grayed value or a *tone* of a hue.

Chroma is the dimension of color which expresses the taste and refinement of the color worker. It is the quality of a color that makes it possible for a certain hue to whisper, shout, or speak in a ladylike tone. It is the property which can give the effect of garishness or elegance to any art expression.

Colors of full intensity are very striking; they form brilliant and interesting accents.

43

Colors of low intensity are subtle and are enjoyed for use in large areas, such as background, floors, and table coverings.

If we look at an arrangement, a table, or a room in full chroma (intense orange—yellow—red—violet) for any length of time, it is fatiguing to the eyes. The eyes rebel against being fatigued; that is a physical fact. Therefore, it is best to use small quantities of strong chroma (full intensity) with large quantities of weaker chroma to achieve a balanced, harmonious picture. Although quantities of full chroma are frequently used successfully in outdoor advertising displays, and in the theatre, where the purpose is to excite and arrest the attention momentarily, it is generally *not* successful when applied to table décor.

How can the chroma of a color be changed? Reduce the intensity of a color through the addition of gray or of its complement. Complementary colors neutralize each other; when mixed in certain proportions they completely destroy one another, or produce gray, which is neutral.

In the case of flowers, which cannot be mixed as paints are mixed, the placement together of similar values or closely related hues tends to reduce intensity. Because grayed hues are neutral, they make excellent backgrounds. For example, the effect of red flowers in red containers can be relieved by using a grayed background. Their intensity can also be reduced if they are seen against a red-orange or orange background.

VIVACIOUS, YET SUBTLE Gray dominates with accents of American beauty. A refreshing contrast of textures and colors is seen in the use of handmade pewter, cranberry crystal, roses, euonymus, and begonia leaves. The charming figures are predominantly gray and green, accented with red. *Arranger: the author.* (Photo: William Sevecke)

Texture also affects chroma. Shiny surfaces reflect light. Dull or pebbly surfaces deflect (spread) light. Contrast in textures adds spark and variety in the use of chroma.

The three dimensions of hue, value, and chroma are needed for the proper understanding of color, just as the three dimensions of length, width, and depth are necessary to describe the exact size of your dining room. If one of these dimensions is omitted, the character of the color is left in doubt. It is possible to vary one quality without disturbing the others.

Chroma may be weakened or strengthened without changing the value or hue.

Hue may be modified without changing the value or chroma.

Value may be changed without affecting the hue or chroma.

Therefore, to describe a color accurately, the hue, the value, and the chroma must be stated. To say turquoise is not enough. It can be specified more clearly by designating it as a light, dark, or medium value of blue-green with a gray tone. If it were *not grayed,* the words *clear* or *intense* could precede *blue-green.*

IMPACT OF COLOR

Color is fantastically exciting. It has the power to create within us certain emotional, physical, and psychological responses. Though we may not all react alike to color, it is generally recognized that certain colors create certain responses. Being aware of this, we can attempt to select the right colors at the right time to say just the right thing.

We know that some colors make us happy and gay; others cause us to feel sad and depressed. There are still others that produce a restful, pleasant experience.

Our physical reactions to color tell us that red, orange, and some yellows appear warm and advancing, while blue, violet, and some greens appear cool and receding.

We react to colors psychologically, physically, and emotionally. Each color has a decided influence and association of its own.

RED. Fire, danger, courage; red is vibrant and attention getting.

BLUE. Quiet, tranquillity, sadness; blue is cool, restful, and induces a sense of serenity. It is soothing to the excitable, but depressing to the sad.

VIOLET. Splendor, regality, dignity; violet combines the warmth of red and the coolness of blue.

YELLOW. Sunshine, cheerfulness; yellow is conducive to a sense of well-being.

ORANGE. Gaiety, excitement; orange is used most successfully as accents.

GREEN. Freshness, relaxation; green is invigorating, a color of nature. It reduces excitement.

PINK and PASTELS. Daintiness; pinks have festive and youthful connotations.

WHITE. Purity, coolness, spirituality; in the prismatic theory, white reflects all colors; in the pigment theory, it is the absence of color.

GRAY. Quiet, noncommittal; it reduces emotional response. It is a mixture of black and white or of other direct complements.

BLACK. Moroseness, fear, smartness, earthiness, sophistication; in the prismatic theory, black absorbs all colors; in the pigment theory, black is the result of the mixture of all colors.

45

Note: White, gray, and black are considered neutral in flower arranging.

COLOR HARMONY

Color harmony is the blending of colors in an orderly fashion to create a feeling of belonging together without producing monotony.

Color harmonies are combinations of colors which are pleasing when seen next to each other. This organized relationship should be well proportioned, varied, and must satisfy the vision and the emotions to be successful.

Color harmonies fall into two general categories: related and contrasted.

RELATED HARMONIES

There are two related harmonies: *monochromatic* and *analogous*. These schemes feature close relationship. They appeal to the emotions and they produce a quiet effect.

MONOCHROMATIC

Mono means one; *chroma* means color: one single hue with its different values and chromas (tints, shades, tones). A monochrome is a gradation or modulation of one hue, no straying to the right or to the left on the color wheel. If you choose blue-violet for your monochrome, be sure not to include either blue or violet as neither has a place in this harmony. They are separate colors which lie to the right and left of blue-violet. Though blue and violet are components of blue-violet, the blending of the two produces a distinct entity which differs from either of the components.

The monochromatic harmony carries with it the possibility of monotony. Therefore, to ensure interest and variety, employ different values, unequal amounts, and unequal intervals. The charm of a monochromatic harmony is its unity.

ANALOGOUS

Analogous colors are neighboring colors on the color wheel, which have a resemblance but which are not the same. Their kinship binds two or more identities otherwise unlike. These adjacent hues are related to each other through one pigment primary.

An analogous color scheme to be interesting should include at least three colors, but should not generally consist of more than one-third of the color wheel. You need not start your analogy with a primary color, nor must a primary be included. You may start with a secondary or tertiary color. However, if a primary is used, your selected colors may go up to, but should not enter, another primary. Unequal intervals between hues and values establish the most satisfying analogy.

CONTRASTED HARMONIES

Contrasted harmonies are the result of combining opposite or near-opposite colors on the color wheel. *Direct complement, split complement, triad,* and *tetrad* are but a few of the possible contrasting harmonies.

Contrasting harmonies appeal to the vision. They are vivid, arresting, and may even

FASHIONED WITH FINESSE
Pale pink conch shell, strawberries, hen and chickens, strawberry foliage, a dramatic ivy branch on a green marble base show the subtle use of complementary hues and the unconventional use of hard and soft textures in this blue-ribbon entry. *Arranger: the author.* (Photo: *The New York Times*)

be startling. If well planned, the result will be harmonious even though the color scheme is contrasted.

DIRECT COMPLEMENTS

Direct complements are harmonies in which two hues directly opposite on the color wheel are used—red and green, blue and orange, violet and yellow. This is the most obvious of all the complements.

SPLIT COMPLEMENTS

Split complements are combinations of three hues: a basic hue with the two hues that lie on either side of its complement. As the term implies, the split divides the complement of a hue into its component parts, using only these parts and omitting the complement. Thus, the "splits" of yellow are red-violet and blue-violet. They are secured by splitting the complement of yellow, which is violet.

A split complement is a harmony of similar colors with a note of opposite color for contrast.

TRIADS

Triadic harmony directs the eye around the color wheel. When three hues are equidistant, forming an equilateral triangle, we have a triadic harmony. Yellow, blue, and red, or green, orange, and violet are triads.

TETRADS

When four colors are equidistant on the color wheel we have a tetrad.

47

Contrasting color schemes are either more lively or more striking than related harmonies. It is well to remember in planning these harmonies to use unequal amounts of color and variety in values and intensities for the most distinguished results.

COLOR AND YOUR TABLE

Do you like color? Is it important to you? If you do, use it by all means. Use it generously if you wish, but use it with care and discretion and know what it can do for you and your table.

Every color goes with every other color if you know the right nuances to use—the right amounts in the right places.

If a *subtle, charming* table is what you desire, choose several values of one color; by using the various tints, tones, and shades of one color, you will create a monochromatic color scheme. Another way of achieving the subtle, charming effect is to use an *analogous* color scheme, with one, two, or three closely related colors, allowing one hue to dominate.

If you wish to create a *dramatic* effect, choose contrasting or near contrasting colors. You might try a scheme in white and black or white and navy blue, punctuated by sharp yellow, chartreuse, orange, or vibrant red.

If you lean toward the *unusual* or *different* and want to achieve something quite offbeat and startling, you can try a combination of chartreuse, violet, and royal blue, or a blending of mustard, blue-green, and orange-red. In using striking color combinations, the law of areas (page 50), which is necessary in all color statements, must be observed most carefully.

If you want a *cool, refreshing* table for a hot day, choose colors in your flowers, food, and accessories that will refresh the eye. Whites, some greens, and ice blues are psychologically cooling.

A NEW LOOK

Dramatize your table with color. Vary the color of your table linens. It is by far the simplest and least expensive way to present a fresh picture while using your same appointments.

Experiment with color. Try your china on a pink cloth; you will find it dainty and charming. On a green cloth it will be refreshing; on a yellow one, bright or gay. An ecru cloth will appear elegant and formal. A white cloth can be effective if it is treated as a color, by using it with bold or contrasting accents, such as ruby red, emerald green, amethyst, or cranberry.

One color harmony should dominate. Too many colors used in equal amounts cause a feeling of busyness and disturb rather than strengthen the unity of the table.

In creating color harmonies for your table, try to plan the more subtle nuances. The more obvious combinations are pedestrian, not always the most artistic.

Blend colors of table appointments. When one hue is used in the appointments, the decorative note can be one of the values of the color, a combination of many colors, or a striking accent.

48

Where different colors are used in china, linens, and glassware, a monochromatic flower arrangement in one of the less dominant colors is preferable.

When multicolored china is used, a solid-color table covering is a good selection. The floral composition should include one or two of the colors found in the china. Or it may repeat the color of the cloth in a lighter or darker value. The color chosen for the cloth should, of course, reflect one of the colors in the china. It is not necessary to repeat every color in the decorative composition that is found in the multicolored china.

Tie-in colors should be echoed in the arrangement. This produces a charming, unified whole, and it is one way of creating a satisfying picture.

A dramatic effect can be achieved when monochromatic or analogous colors are used in your table appointments and a contrasting color or colors are selected for your decorative composition. Be sure, however, when using a color in contrast to your appointments to have a definite relationship in texture and spirit. The contrasting color or colors do not detract from, but on the contrary, serve to create, a dramatic feeling of dominance in the appointments and an over-all unity.

You can try to match colors to a fault. For example, a pale blue cloth, china, crystal, and a pale blue flower arrangement certainly seem to lack vitality. The repetition of the same color produces a feeling of dominance, but dominance without contrast can be uninspired and commonplace.

LIGHT SPEAKS

In addition to texture and color, light must be considered for any artistic result. All three are interdependent and cannot be perceived or understood separately. For maximum artistic success *colors should be blended, textures varied,* and *lighting mixed.* For superior results, color must be considered in relation to both the proper light and the appropriate textures.

Example 1. Colors appear different under different lighting. Under incandescent light (yellow light), blues and violets lose their identity; reds become flame. Pinks and pastels are most pleasant under yellow light.

Example 2. Dip scraps of velvet, satin, and cotton in the same dye bath. The satin will appear brighter than the cotton because its shiny surface reflects the light. The velvet will appear darker because its high-pile texture absorbs the light.

Example 3. Take the same fabrics from one room to another room, or from a far wall to a window, and it will be easy to observe the variations in color depending upon the light.

DESIGN IN COLOR

All colors are pleasing if properly used. The principles of design (Chapter 5) apply not only to line but also to color. Combining the right colors in the right quantity, in the proper values, and in the proper chromatic steps according to the principles of design provides the yardstick we use to arrive at a desired effect.

49

LAW OF AREAS

Without becoming too technical, we all are aware of the tremendous force of bright colors. Therefore, bright colors should be used with the utmost care if the result is to be beautiful. A good rule to follow is this: Whenever large quantities or areas of color are used, make sure that the color is quiet or of low intensity. The greater the area or the amount of color used, the nearer the intensity should come toward gray. The smaller the area to be covered, the brighter the color may be.

In a broad sense we may say that *color balances at neutral gray*. That is, a moderate amount of strong color may be balanced by the right amount of grayer color. Small bits of powerful color may be used to balance large fields of weak chroma. For example, a spot of reddish purple may be balanced by a field of gray-green.

This is called the Law of Areas. This law is the foundation upon which all color work is based and is extremely important.

ACCENT AND BALANCE

Every color scheme, whether for your home, your wardrobe, or your table, needs the contrast of something bright, something dull, something dark, or something light for interest and variety.

Color has the power of attraction. It increases or decreases the sense of space. It gives a feeling of weight and size. Dark or intense colors appear heavier, and a small quantity can balance a larger quantity of light color.

Contrasting colors are used to emphasize, not compete with, the dominant color harmony. Therefore, small quantities should be used. A bit of shocking pink (violet red) can accent or relieve the monotony of a large area of pale pink or light lavender, orange, gray-green, or blue-green.

Contrast can be stated by a change of hue, value (a dark accent on a light field, and vice versa), or chroma (a bright or intense bit combined with a grayed area). Contrast does much to unify the dominant color. It is the spark which adds distinction and transforms monotony into harmony.

The importance of color cannot be minimized. It is woven into our every activity and thought. We meet it every day in fashions, foods, home decorating, science, industry, and art. Do you ever wonder why some advertisements attract our attention more than others? I am sure if you would stop to analyze it you would find that the dramatic impact of color or the color combinations was the thing that first attracted your attention rather than the text. Color causes you to stop and look. In the same way, a bedroom decorated in pastels (pinks and violets) would bring a subtle response; you would sense that the room was charming even before you appraised the individual pieces in the room.

Because color can produce whatever effect one desires, it is essential to understand something of its power and possibilities. Color adds character to a well-co-ordinated table setting. Through color you can express elegance, refinement, gay sophistication, or create any image you wish.

Part Two

Chapter 7

ETIQUETTE AND FASHIONS

New occasions teach new duties,
Time makes ancient good uncouth.
JAMES RUSSELL LOWELL

COURTESY and common sense are the backbone of good etiquette. Etiquette reflects the dictates or usages of polite society. It reflects gentility, fashion, vogue, or the order of the day.

Eating is an elemental fact of life. It has sustained people everywhere since the days of Adam and Eve. Though the foods we eat may be similar, the way we eat them and how we present them make the difference. The pleasures and graces of eating have been given increased attention as peoples have progressed.

Today much thought is given to the selection and preparation of good food. However, a hostess is as often judged by the table she sets as by the food she serves. The manner in which the food is served and the presentation are the amenities that add immeasurable beauty and grace to the art of dining.

Contrary to common belief, the rules of etiquette have not been laid down by any one social arbiter. In reality, customs and conventions arise from the way people live in a certain place at a given time.

An Englishman eats pie with a spoon and fork, whereas the American uses a fork. In some countries it is polite practice to mop up the last drop of gravy in a plate with a piece of bread. If your host should select a morsel of choice food from his own plate and place it on yours, you would, I am sure, be shocked; yet in a Chinese home it would be considered the highest compliment.

As you can see, sometimes the height of good manners in one place may be the opposite of good manners in another. It is well to remember that what we consider good form is only so in relation to the traditions and habits of polite society in which we live. That is why many customs of the past are no longer part of our way of living. Instead, they are being replaced by customs which express our present attitudes.

In table settings the manner of presentation is still important. As everyone knows, etiquette not only contributes to the convenience and consideration for others, but also transforms mere eating into gracious dining.

How to Set Your Table

It is important to know the correct placement of appointments—what goes where on the table. There are only a few basic rules in setting a table that remain constant. Other rules vary with the type of living and the occasion (see photographs on pages 24, 27, and 123).

Flatware. Place knives, sharp edge toward plate, and spoons at the right of the plate. Forks are placed at the left, all in order of their use, starting from the outside toward the plate. Oyster forks, however, are placed on the right with the spoons.

Glassware. Goblets go directly above the knife and spoon. Wine glasses are lined up at the right of the goblet.

China. Bread-and-butter plates go above the forks at the left, with the butter knife placed horizontally across the plate, cutting edge facing forward. In formal settings, bread-and-butter plates are omitted. If salad is to be served with the main course, salad plates are placed to the left of the forks.

Napkins are placed, neatly folded, at the left of the setting. In formal settings, napkins are often placed on the service plates.

Napkins, silver, and china should be about one inch from the edge of the table.

When doilies are used, they are placed at the edge or about one-half inch from the edge of the table, with equal spaces between settings. Allow at last 20 to 24 inches between settings to avoid crowding and to facilitate serving.

The centerpiece should be low enough not to hinder conversation.

Candles should be above or below eye level and should not be the same height as the floral arrangement (see photographs on pages 24 and 27).

Formality

To speak of formality one must first understand the philosophy and thinking of a people during a certain time.

In America, at the turn of the century, distinct class differences were apparent. Many writers covering the history of that era refer to the upper class, the upper middle class, lower middle class, and lower class. The two extremes—the most and the least affluent—represented the majority. People were either very rich or very poor, and their financial status governed their social standing and the manner in which they lived. The more affluent people were, the more they conformed to the rigid standards of their established society. Slavish adherence to formality was indeed the custom, which was followed to the

54

letter. Living was on a lavish scale among the wealthy, and ostentation and ornateness were prevalent in the frivolous Gay Nineties.

A gradual evolution has taken place in our country in the past forty to fifty years, and the austere simplicity of the war years has gradually disappeared.

Economically in the past twenty years the standard of living has risen. Opportunities have opened in every field for anyone who has the vision and the ability to fill a job. It is no longer necessary to be the son or grandson of a railroad magnate or the owner of an oil or steel company to become its president. The great upper class and the extreme lower class are no longer the majority of our population. Today more people have more things, and more people have greater opportunities for learning and culture. Many, indeed, have taken advantage of this to make life fuller and more pleasant.

Philosophically, our contemporary attitude is one of directness and smartness. Imaginative expressions of beauty are reflected through functional, stylized simplicity and elegance.

Formality in Table Setting

Formality in table setting varies greatly from strict formality, rarely practiced in America today, to casual informality. There are many degrees between these extremes on the scale of formality. And, like the colors of the rainbow, there is also an overlapping. Only the extremes seem well defined. The twentieth-century mode of dining is neither extremely formal nor completely lacking in some form. For even in the most informally planned setting today you will find style, order, and good taste.

DEGREE OF FORMALITY

The time of day does not always indicate the formality of the meal. Though most gala and important occasions are celebrated in the evening, there is no rule that indicates that all evening functions must be formal and that likewise all luncheons must be informal. Two examples are wedding breakfasts and engagement luncheons.

The degree of formality has to do with the occasion, the appointments, and the service. The home, the dining room, and the furnishings establish the type of living, but the occasion regulates the formality within that scope.

CLASSIFICATIONS OF SERVICE

To understand better this vague and flexible subject, we will divide it into three accepted categories: formal, informal, and semiformal. Although it is difficult to be definite, these classifications of service cover the whole field of dining from the simplest luncheon to the most elaborate dinner.

Formality means observance of social forms in accordance with established customs and etiquette. The formal table must be scrupulously exact in details; it must be ceremonious, impressive, and orderly.

A formal table implies the use of appointments rich in texture and quality, precision in placement of china, crystal, silver, napkins, and accessories. Wine glasses are used, as are candles or candelabra—all according to the established traditional form. The twentieth century's contribution to the formal setting is the now acceptable use of exquisite doilies. See the Marghab Linen Collection at the Metropolitan Museum of Art.

A formal table must reflect dignity and elegance. Formal service, which must accompany a formal meal, must be proper and precise. A number of servants or footmen are required for such service. This type of strictly formal service is seldom practiced in our contemporary dining at home. It may be seen on rare occasions in society and, more frequently, at official government functions for visitors when royalty and dignitaries are guests.

As soon as one departs from the formal pattern, the question of formality or informality becomes one of degree.

Semiformal means any slight deviation from the established form, generally in the matter of service. A semiformal table is one that observes many of the practices that stem from the formal table, except the most strictly technical facets. There are many degrees of semiformality. Nevertheless, attention to detail, aesthetic refinement in appointments, service, design, and food must be observed.

A few ways in which the semiformal occasion differs from the formal one are: service plates are optional; bread-and-butter plates, ash trays, cigarettes and matches may be used; fewer servants are required; there are fewer courses; and service is more relaxed.

Informal means not in the usual or regular form; without ceremony, casual. The informal table usually involves the use of things of different origin. Twentieth-century appointments are tasteful and smart, but not elaborate. They may match or be combined for either utility or effect. The service and design of an informal table should be planned for ease and comfort. The setting should give a relaxed, casual appearance of warm, friendly hospitality.

Appointments for an informal setting should always be functional. If your appointments are not very distinguished in pattern, shape, or quality, or if you lack the needed quantity, color can be a boon. Added appointments can be co-ordinated by an organized color scheme. This can be created either through your table covering or through the decorative unit (see Chapters 3–8).

Place mats, so adaptable, can be simple or elaborate, and the bare table is smart and in good taste.

There is a wide variety of expression within the scale of informality, just as there is within the scope of semiformality. It is sometimes difficult to tell where one begins and ends.

Styles and Types of Table Setting

Style is a characteristic mode of presentation. It is the prevailing fashion of a specific era. It is the result of emphasis within a certain period, and many things are particular to that certain period. For example, the rock and shell (*rocaille*) motif, classical elegance,

COLOR SINGS Fortissimo colors of the distinctive figurines and plant material are a rich and unifying contrast to the subtle hues of the appointments. *Arranger: the author.*

VARIED SIMILITUDE An arrangement need not be alike on both sides. Basic plant material (clivia foliage, philodendron hostatum and dubae and ivy leaves) unifies the design. Diverse accents create surprise and excitement. Violet-green echeveria and black grapes. Reverse side of the vase: red anthurium and green grapes. *Arranger: the author.* (Photo: William Sevecke)

and delicacy in color and style typify the French rococo period of Louis XV and eighteenth-century France. The classic designs of formal grandeur, rich colors, and Oriental accents are some expressions of the Georgian period in England and America (George I, II, and III). Austere simplicity, bright colors, charm, and practical appointments reflect our seventeenth-century Colonial America.

The twentieth century is and has been a period of freedom and new concepts throughout most of the world. Designs are striking, bold, and venturesome. Materials are different, ideas unprecedented. The journals of history will no doubt note these individual expressions that characterize twentieth-century styles in America, Denmark, Italy, and elsewhere.

Today's table settings represent generally three styles: Traditional or Classic, Contemporary, and Modern.

MAGNIFICENT REPLICA Treasured antiques—French Louis XV candelabra, bronze ormolu bowl, Rhine wine glasses and finger bowls (Baccarat), Limoges place plates, and luxurious Scalamandré silk celadon table covering—re-create the spirit of the French rococo period. The classic treatment of the centerpiece of freesias, ranunculuses, white lilacs, pansies, roses, vines further adds the elegant traditional touch. *Arranger: Mrs. Carlton Vandewarker.* (Photo: William Sevecke)

TRADITIONAL OR CLASSIC TABLE SETTING

The traditional setting reflects the fashion of a past period, usually employing antiques. A traditional table may be assembled with authentic antique appointments or may be set with reproductions. The spirit of the table can best be translated through the consistent relationship of all appointments and accessories belonging to a particular period.

The decorative composition should echo the past. You should use a traditional container. Know how to create a good design in order to achieve the most artistic result, but retain the spirit and mode of the particular period.

CONTEMPORARY TABLE SETTING

This style is an expression of today's living, which successfully combines present-day accoutrements and accessories with those from past periods or past influences (Japan, China). It shows a respect for tradition and adapts it to present-day living. It also involves the use of old appointments in a present-day setting. The influence of classic simplicity plus a note of elegance brings designs of streamlined serenity to modern living.

Simplicity, beauty, and practicality are some of the essentials in contemporary table décor. Equally important are smartness, imagination, and distinction. All these qualities manifest themselves in the appointments and in the organization of design.

The decorative composition should incorporate the best features of restrained linear simplicity inspired by Oriental art, combined with a greater abundance of plant material and the freer use of rich color derived from Occidental art, appropriate to the setting.

MODERN TABLE SETTING

Modern means existing at the moment, fresh, crisp, novel, just produced, the latest fashion or innovation. It shows creativeness and a characteristic difference that distinguishes it from former or classical times.

In modern table décor and flower arrangement the idea and the treatment deviate strikingly from traditions of the past. However, the bizarre should be discouraged and the beautiful encouraged.

The characteristics of modern American table settings are seen in the choice of clear-cut plant forms, striking contrasts, strong, rich colors or subtle nuances, dramatic designs of stylized simplicity—integrated with space. The use of space is very important in modern expressions. For example, many dining tables are bare, exposing the beautifully finished wood. Equipment and accessories show orginality in materials and design and are smart and functional. The floral composition and the whole setting must be uncluttered and forcefully portray dramatic simplicity, creativeness, and distinction.

There are various types of table settings: breakfast, lunch, dinner, tea, and supper are types of meals that may be served either seated, buffet, or upon trays.

58

A BRIGHT GOOD MORNING Charming, delicate pastel colors permeate the setting in this perky pink breakfast room. Pink linen scalloped doilies (plastic), Danish white and blue china. An arrangement of euonymus, dracaena sandriana, pink geraniums, carnations, and funkia foliage in a blue and white Delft compote is gracefully gay. *Arranger: Mrs. Joseph Cooper.* (Photo: William Sevecke)

SOPHISTICATED LUNCHEON Classic modern china, delicately traced in shadowy gray and gold (Wood Nymph by Rosenthal); gray and silver-banded place mats; and emerald green glass are knowingly co-ordinated to emphasize the sculptured arrangement. Golden callas, dracaena, messangèana, funkia, and galax highlight a copper-green Young Myth. *Arranger: the author.* (Photo: William Allen)

BREAKFAST TABLE

Set your breakfast table with a colorful cloth or doilies that will say a bright "good morning." Simple patterned china in light colors is best, nothing elaborate. The decorative note should be informal and gay.

BREAKFAST TRAY

Use dainty appointments in related delicate colors and a small, low flower arrangement. If there is insufficient room, a single blossom or a corsage will add a cheerful note. Make sure your tray is large enough to hold the necessary utensils without crowding.

LUNCHEON TABLE

The same general conditions in table setting should be observed for a luncheon as for an informal dinner, with a few differences.

Candles are not used for luncheons, except for wedding breakfasts, engagement luncheons, or in a room where there is no daylight.

The selection of appointments depends upon the degree of formality and the occasion. An impressive occasion requires your best china, crystal, silver, and linens. Medium-sized napkins and luncheon plates are used.

Informal luncheons endorse the use of contrasting colors, textured or colorful table coverings, earthenware or pottery. A simple fruit, vegetable, or flower arrangement accents the color and sustains the interest of the setting.

Luncheons are generally more informal than dinners, but not always. Bread-and-butter plates, ash trays, cigarettes and matches, which are incorrect for a formal dinner, are perfectly correct for the most elaborate luncheon, as is a soup cup instead of the more formal soup plate.

DINNER TABLE

The friendly glow of candlelight adds sparkle to your glassware, gives glamour to your setting, and contributes greatly to a festive mood—the atmosphere every hostess tries to create. The setting, the service, and the food are the essentials which indicate the formality or informality of the meal.

Formal dinners require a number of servants for proper service; exquisite china and crystal; table covering of damask, fine linen, organdy, or lace; beautiful silver in flatware, candelabra, and compotes; service plates, wine glasses, and finger bowls.

Informal dinners follow the pattern of the informal luncheon. Some of the essential differences between an informal luncheon table and an informal dinner table are the dinner-size napkins, the dinner plates, and the use of candles.

BUFFET TABLE

The gay and relaxing service of a buffet table is the simplest and most popular way of entertaining a large number of guests at home. With limited space and a shortage of help, this way of entertaining for dinner, brunch, Sunday-night supper, or after the theatre is both practical and fun.

Your table may be placed against the wall or windows, allowing greater floor space for your guests to move about. Whether your table is placed against the wall or in the center of the room, the food should be conveniently arranged. Hot dishes, casseroles, and the like, in particular, should be placed around the forward portion of the table in logical sequence, where they are easily accessible. Napkins (neatly and simply folded), silver, china, and other serving dishes should be grouped to create balance.

In making your arrangement, allow your originality and ingenuity full sway. The more unusual the containers, accessories, plant material, and design, the more exciting the result. The size of the arrangement is guided and limited by its relation to the size of the table and the size of the room.

CASUAL YET SMART   Functional appointments and high-voltage colors make this a stunning informal buffet. Aqua and white fringed cloth, teakwood salad bowl, blue-green goblets, charcoal-brown-banded plates, pottery casserole, aqua and green napkins. Arrangement in blond sculptured wood: pandanus, tritoma, orange lilies, orange to orange-red zinnias, and funkia foliage. The professional touch is evident in the meticulous co-ordination of color, texture, and spirit. *Arranger: the author.* (Photo: William Allen)

Buffet service is acknowledged as an informal type of service. However, the table setting, appointments, and accessories, and social amenities may range from formal elegance to casual informality, depending on the occasion and the background décor, making your buffet setting itself formal, semiformal, or informal.

The buffet is your opportunity for free artistic expression. Let your buffet table vibrate with your individuality through color and design. Make it an expression of tasteful, friendly hospitality.

Buffet tables may be set either symmetrically or asymmetrically. Group your plates, silver, and napkins to create the feeling of balance that is so important in this type of setting. The floral composition may be placed in the center, center back, side back, or at the ends of the table. Candles, candelabra, and accessories may be used for both interest and balance. Serving platters, casseroles, salad bowls, and/or chafing dishes must be distributed to retain balance. Do not overcrowd your table; spaces facilitate self-service and make the food and decorative units more important.

Step back from your table; if the over-all picture is one of equilibrium, the chances are good design has been achieved.

KINDS OF BUFFETS

There are several kinds of buffets: lap service, seated self-service, and semibuffet.

Lap service. The buffet table holds all the food and equipment and the floral arrangement, the guests help themselves, and they balance their plates on their laps. This type of service is useful for potluck suppers, cocktail parties, and spur-of-the-moment celebrations.

Seated self-service. The buffet table is set with the food and decorative unit only. Small tables seating four, six, or eight persons are each set with silver, china, crystal, napkins, salts and peppers, cigarette dishes, ash trays, and a well-co-ordinated decorative arrangement. If the tables are large enough, candles may also be used; if the table is crowded, a candle or candles with foliage at the base and just a few flowers could add interest, leaving the table nicely balanced and uncluttered. This is the type of buffet setting and service we use most frequently today.

Semibuffet. The table is arranged as for a seated meal, complete with the appropriate centerpiece. A first course, if planned, may be on the table. The main course should be attractively arranged on the side buffet where the guests then help themselves. The table may be cleared by a servant, or guests may place the appointments from the finished course on a serving cart.

TEA TABLE

Afternoon tea has long been regarded as an English custom. But of late more Americans are happily emulating their English cousins. Tea time—or coffee time, if you prefer—provides an oasis of peace and relaxation in our busy schedules.

Teas may be simple and intimate for four, six, or a dozen people, or they may be elaborate and large where hundreds of people attend.

Generally, the appointments (except for a very informal occasion) should be lovely

62

ENGAGEMENT TEA The romantic occasion is highlighted by an enchanting and practical arrangement on a silver candelabrum—so appropriate for this or any special occasion. Arrangement: Euonymus, inkberry (Ilex glabra), pink carnations, lily of the valley, spirea, white and green funkia, pink tulle, and pink satin ribbons. Appointments: a dainty white embroidered dacron cloth over a pink liner, white porcelain, an English silver tea service, and white linen napkins. *Arranger: the author.* (Photo: William Sevecke)

and dainty. A cloth of either fine linen, nylon, organdy that is embroidered or appliquéd, or one of Alençon or Point de Venice lace, in pastels, ivory, or white, is most appropriate. An overhang of about 18 inches adds grace and beauty to the setting.

Teacups and dessert plates should be fine china, delicate in design and pattern. Some of the cups and saucers may be placed on a silver tray with the tea service. If there is not enough room on the tray, they may be placed on the table next to the tea service. Balance should be kept in mind in distributing the candelabra, tea service or services, floral decoration, food, dessert plates, cups and saucers, and napkins, which are 11 to 12 inches in size.

Tea table appointments must be nicely distributed, well spaced, and uncrowded, to show off their beauty. A successful tea table is fresh, inviting, and charming.

TV TRAYS

Television has not only affected our entertainment, but has also influenced some of our entertaining and dining habits in the home. In many cities and communities it has all but dominated both. Meals are planned in front of the television so as not to miss a particular program. With this compelling medium commanding our attention frequently at mealtime, a new innovation—the snack or TV tray—has become very popular. These trays come with their own folding legs or braces, which make them both practical and convenient.

Tray service can be very attractive. It usually is comfortable and expedient. Both the setting and the menu should be simple to facilitate serving. Plate service, practical essential appointments, and gay linens must all be carefully co-ordinated in color, texture, and informal spirit, because the area is so small and leaves no room for discord.

Plate service is desirable for most tray meals, but particularly so for the family. It is quick, it is easy—both considerations in this type of service. With the fondness for entertaining guests informally, however, tray service has leaped to our attention. When having guests, the trays may be either covered with mats or left bare. Each tray may be set with the appointments and with a small corsage or boutonniere for special occasions.

If you prefer, a small buffet table can be arranged from which the guests may help themselves to the food (generally a salad or a casserole on a hot tray) and equipment. Flatware for the meal can be rolled into a gaily colored napkin—so easy to carry with the dinner plate back to the tray. Bread-and-butter plates are unnecessary. A salad bowl should be used only if the tray is large. It is preferable to use a large dinner plate that will hold everything. A bread basket may be passed.

A teacart nearby is convenient when removing soiled dishes after the finished course.

The dessert, appointments, and coffeepot (electric) should be organized beforehand, to save time and many trips to the kitchen.

Things that make a tray attractive are: a smart, gay color scheme; individual appointments related in texture and informal in mood; an original and co-ordinated menu that is planned in advance and easy to serve; and a small distinctive floral, fruit, or vegetable decoration. Although there is not much room for a sizable floral decoration on each tray, try a small arrangement, using Oasis covered with tinfoil in which fresh greens and a few blooms can be arranged, or make a small corsage. Place your decoration at the far left corner of the tray, or pin it onto the rolled napkin.

For example, on St. Valentine's Day a little nosegay would be charming for the ladies. And at Christmas some small Christmas balls and a small spray of greens, some holly and berries, or desert juniper would add a festive note.

A clothespin painted or sprayed with enamel or flat paint makes an unusual holder for a corsage or a few flowers arranged artistically. It can be clipped to the side of the tray.

GARDEN TRAYS

Garden tray luncheons and suppers can follow many of the preceding suggestions. Keep in mind the suitability of the appointments you use. For outdoors, pottery, wood, metal, and sturdy tumblers are good choices. Table coverings, either cloths or mats, of coarse-textured or woven fabrics or plastics in bright or contrasting colors, are fitting. The arrangement should be low, and garden flowers are appropriate.

Chapter 8

THE DECORATIVE UNIT

fLOWER arrangement is the organization of design and color toward beauty. Sparked by a beguiling idea and impeccable craftsmanship, an arrangement might truly become an artistic masterpiece.

The decorative unit is often called the centerpiece, but it is not always used in the center of the table. It may be placed at the ends, center back, corners, or at either side of the back of the table in balanced symmetry. Your centerpiece may be composed of either flowers, foliage, plants, fruits, or vegetables, used separately or in combination with other plant materials or with accessories, such as candles, candelabra, figurines, and compotes.

GRACE AND SENSITIVITY Forsythia, red-orange peony tulips, croton leaves on a gold column are superbly crafted in this fluid design, which emphasizes rhythm and contrast in forms, textures, colors, and spatial voids. Arrangement is particularly appropriate for the back or ends of a table. *Arranger: the author.* (Photo: David L. Steindler)

When planning your centerpiece, keep in mind its twofold purpose: to *enhance* and to *unify* the whole setting. A good centerpiece also must have unity and variety within itself. The centerpiece must therefore be related to either the china, linen, or crystal in color, texture, and spirit. The centerpiece need not include all the colors in all the appointments or even all the colors in multicolored china, as long as a dominant effect is achieved. This can be done by selecting one color and its values. If more than one color is used, one must dominate while the others should be subordinated in order to avoid conflict (see Chapter 6).

It is also possible to create a harmonious effect by co-ordinating linen, china, and crystal and by using your decorative composition as a spotlight contrast. For example, visualize the co-ordinated appointments of an Alençon lace cloth, ivory and gold-band china, gold-rim crystal goblets, gilt candelabrum, crystal and gilt compotes, and Dirilyte flatware, accented by the striking note of Better Times or Happiness roses. The elegant table appointments are related in color, texture, and quality. The roses, which are suitable in texture and mood, provide a striking contrast in color. This direct opposition in color is not only exciting, but also serves to unify the dominant elements, thus creating a dramatic table. Contrast is like a catalyst—its very presence makes all the other elements run together to create dominance. Contrast makes a table scintillate; it brings the table alive.

Most tables are viewed from all sides. An exception is a table placed against a wall or window, in which case the centerpiece may be placed at either end or center back. Decorative units must therefore be properly finished all around. This is not nearly so difficult as most people believe, since all sides do not necessarily have to be alike. It does, however, require more plant material and a little more time than an arrangement which will be viewed only from the front.

Technique

PLACEMENT

One of the first things to consider in making your table arrangement is where it is going to be placed—in the center, off center, at the end or ends, the corners, or center back. Your originality, innate sense of balance, knowledge of design, and the number of guests you plan to serve will determine the most attractive and convenient placement. For example, with an uneven number of guests the floral composition may be placed at one end and the settings around the other three sides.

SIZE OF DECORATIVE COMPOSITION

The size of the composition is in direct relationship to the size and shape of the table and, in turn, suggests the proper-size container. The composition or centerpiece should be neither so small as to look insignificant on a large table nor so large as to be overpowering, dipping into the food and interfering with the appointments and service. It should be important enough to add a note of interest to the setting without impeding the service or disturbing the view or conversation of your guests.

HEIGHT FOR A SEATED MEAL

Flower arrangements should generally be low. As the table increases in size and number of place settings, it is logical that the decorative composition increase in size in order to be in proper scale and proportion. As a guide, and a guide only, the height of an arrangement for a seated dinner should generally not exceed 18 inches. I believe this to be a good approximation. However, let us not be too rigid or precise, but rather be sensible, in arriving at the height of our compositions.

I have seen a flower arrangement that was so heavily massed, without any voids, that it was quite impossible to see or talk to the guests on the opposite side of the table. It spread across the table, touching appointments and food. I have also seen others that may have been slightly taller than the suggested maximum height, composed of pussy willows, Scotch broom, flowering branches, or other light materials, having an airy silhouette. They did not interfere in any way with the vision or conversation. So you can see how important it is to use the stated approximate height only as a guide.

SPRING PREVIEW Magnolia branches, buds, blossoms, and foliage are superbly crafted in a design capturing the poetry of spring. *Arranger: the author.* (Photo: George J. Hirsch)

LENGTH OF AN ARRANGEMENT

For a six-foot table the length of an arrangement should be approximately 20 to 24 inches. Candles and accessories contribute to the length and weightiness and should be considered when planning the size of your composition.

In setting a formal table for twelve or more guests, ample space should be allowed between settings (about 24 inches). The flower arrangement is then placed between settings. In that way it does not interfere with the nodding view across the table. Conversation at large formal dinners is directed toward guests at either side, not across the table. The decorative arrangement therefore may be proportionately large, but must remain in good scale and proportion to the table. Always view the finished composition for a seated dinner from a seated position, as your guests will.

SIZE OF A BUFFET ARRANGEMENT

Your buffet arrangement is determined by the size of the table, the size of the room, the height of the ceiling, and the location of the table. It may be larger and more dramatic than for a seated meal, but must be in good scale and proportion to its container, the table, and the room. Review your finished composition just as your guests will do, standing.

Be a little daring in choosing and combining your plant material, container, and accessories—in color and design. Use your imagination if you want your buffet table to be smart and different.

TEA TABLE ARRANGEMENT

At most teas, guests either stand or sit at small tables at some distance from the tea table. Tea is a gentle, light repast, and the decorative arrangement should be in keeping with the spirit and the setting. The arrangement may be taller, since the guests are not seated at the serving table.

Making the Arrangement

Flower arranging is a stimulating art. Because it is fun and truly easy to master, it is one of the most satisfying and gratifying of the creative arts. For those who have recently been introduced to this art of flower arranging, the following remarks, I hope, will prove helpful.

Flower arranging is not a haphazard placing of a bunch of flowers in a container without thought. It is first seeing the form, line, pattern, texture, and color of the plant material, then recognizing its potentials in creating a beautiful design, which help you execute what you have in mind (see Chapter 5).

Plant material, container, and mechanical aids are the essential elements of a flower arrangement.

68

DRAMATIC SIMPLICITY   Striking structural outline, distinctive Polynesian statuette and interesting focal material are uniquely co-ordinated to create dimensional balance and a feeling of oneness. Sansevieria, cocculus, aralia and aralia foliage, pineapple, echeveria, and grapes. For a seated dinner remove sansevieria and tall cocculus. *Arranger: the author.* (Photo: William Sevecke)

FRAGILE MOOD Graceful branches of budding forsythia and yellow iris in a bronze usabata on a Japanese burl reflect simplicity and restraint in an Oriental manner. *Arranger: the author.* (Photo: William Sevecke)

PLANT MATERIAL

Arrangements can be easily organized when varied forms in plant material are selected and combined. For instance, you will find all of any one kind of plant material—round or spiky—a problem. Keep this in mind when looking for your plant material.

For your *structure* or *outline* select branches, buds, or any slender plant material. This type of material is referred to as *line material.*

Round, more solid forms, generally in darker colors, are successful when used for emphasis or accent. This type of plant material is often called *focal material.*

Other plant material, not quite so delicate as the line material or so weighty as the focal material, is used between the two in order to create an easy transition from the very delicate outline to the heavy focal area. This material is called *intermediate* or *secondary material.*

Establish your main line by selecting a long line for your first placement. This line should be approximately one and a half to twice the width of a low bowl plus its height, or one and a half to twice the height of a tall container.

Next, develop your outline or structural pattern, which may evolve from the basic art forms: the *cube,* the *sphere,* and the *pyramid.* A division of any one of these or a combination of more than one can serve to create your skeletal outline. A few of the possibilities for varied structural designs are vertical; horizontal; L-shape; crescent; spiral; oval; Hogarth, or parabolic curve; and equilateral, isosceles, or scalene triangle. Reinforce your structural outline with intermediate material, the intermediate material to follow the established line or lines. In placing your linear material, remember that the voids (spaces) add interest and variety to design. Keep the intermediate material shorter than the outline. Place it so it will both broaden the line and create depth. This is done by adding some plant material to the side, some in back, and some directly in front of the main line or lines, being sure not to obliterate or confuse your main or structural design. The placement of the structural outline with its solids and voids must always be in good visual balance in order to create a feeling of equilibrium and repose. The voids must be varied and uneven in order to produce a distinguished silhouette.

There is an area in the arrangement where all the lines appear to meet. At this area the larger, darker forms are used to create emphasis. The size, position, color, and weight of these concentrated forms command attention. They draw the attention from the structural outline to the center of interest, holding the attention momentarily (if the focal area is just right)—thus unifying the design.

It would be interesting to experiment by creating a design omitting the focal area. The eye would wander up, down, and around the outline, having no place to rest. Thus the composition as a whole would lack emphasis and unity.

The more lines used in creating a design, the more concentrated and emphatic the focal area should be, in order to achieve balance and unity. With fewer lines the focal area should be smaller and less important.

Even though the focal area serves to unify the design and draw the eye temporarily to its momentary resting place, it should always be subtly woven into the design; it should not be an unrelated, bold, or blatant bull's-eye.

The old adage "Practice makes perfect" is applicable to flower arranging. But who is to say what is perfect? How do we know when we have reached perfection? Perfection is somewhat like beauty. It is intangible and relative, not a mathematical equation. It is a visual ideal in the eye and mind of the beholder. Practice makes for proficiency. As we become more proficient our standards rise and so does our visual ideal of perfection.

The important thing in any creative art is to get started. If your first attempts are disappointing, do not be discouraged. You will find that with practice and with each succeeding venture you become more confident and more competent. One idea leads to another, making flower arranging an exciting, growing, creative art that can bring pleasure to everyone.

CONTAINERS

Broadly speaking, anything that holds the plant material within designated, fixed limits may be a container. More usually, however, it is a receptacle that holds water.

Containers are made of pottery, porcelain, silver, crystal, wood, alabaster, plastic, and metal, just to mention a few. Bowls, dishes, trays, compotes, tureens, epergnes, plaques, baskets, scales, stove tops, and driftwood are some suggested types and styles which are appropriate for dining tables. Variety in containers is endless.

A well-chosen container should never dominate the composition. Elaborate, highly ornamented, blatant, or multicolored containers distract from the major interest, the plant material. If you select a simple container or one that is classical in form, quiet or neutral in color, you will find it most adaptable.

71

CONVENTIONAL AND UNCONVENTIONAL CONTAINERS ABOVE, brass tray, crystal and gilt, composition cup, chartreuse epergne, metal lamp base, pottery dish, enamel-on-brass bowl, pottery boat. (Photo: William Sevecke)

BELOW, left, an English silver biscuit box; center, sterling silver compote with grape design (Jensen); and right, revolving tureen, English, silver plated. (Photo: William Sevecke)

For the unusual, use your imagination. Adapt or convert things not usually associated with flowers (see Chapter 9). For example, try an old gilt frame, a clock case, a cigar or cigarette box, a silver biscuit box, or a tripod from a Bunsen burner. These original ideas make unexpected and charming conversation pieces. Anything goes!

Bases often give that needed lift to low, flat containers and plaques. They often give the arrangement a graceful air by improving the over-all proportion and balance of the composition. Be sure to use bases only when they do so. Many containers have their own bases and do not require additional ones.

MECHANICAL AIDS

It is said that a good workman is as good as his tools. The proper tools or mechanical aids can be a great help. The structure, grace, and stability of an arrangement depend in a measure upon the use of good mechanics. And a good craftsman selects the most suitable aids for each type of arrangement. The following are some of the most important and most popular mechanical aids.

72

Holders: vary in shape and size. *Pin* or *needle-point holders* should have long sharp pins, close together, secured in a heavy base. I feel these are generally the most useful, but other types are also available, such as *hairpin holders* and the *cage-type holder,* which are useful for heavy branches. The *cup pinholder* is a boon for plaques, driftwood, or containers that do not hold water.

Cutting tools: clippers, florist knife, scissors (long-handled Japanese type).

Wire: thin, medium, and heavy; chicken wire; flat Twistems; new, round plant ties that come on a 250-foot roll.

Hardware cloth (ratwire): use around driftwood, manzanita, and echeveria, to raise and to impale securely.

Clay and paraffin: anchor holder.

Tapes: floral tape: green, brown, white, orchid; *masking tape:* white, beige, and in colors; *tuck tape:* green; is least affected by moisture; will stick to Styrofoam; *translucent adhesive tape; transparent Scotch tape.*

Toothpicks: round, wooden, natural, and colored (not plastic); for fruit and vegetable arrangements. *Florist picks:* green, with or without wire attached; several sizes; excellent for fruit arrangements or to reinforce stems.

Test tubes: varied sizes and shapes; useful for blossoms in a fruit and vegetable arrangement or to raise a bud or flower whose stem may have broken. To achieve proper height, attach tube securely to stick or bare branch of the required length by winding with tuck tape or floral tape.

Plumber's lead: pliable metal; can be purchased from a plumber or plumbing supply store. Cut two pieces of lead five or six inches long and three-quarters of an inch wide, crisscross one over the other, wire securely together. Use in tall container by placing one end in the vase and folding the opposite end over the back of the vase. This leaves the two crossbars free to secure the main lines and hold the material in place.

MECHANICAL AIDS   Oasis, holders, Gard-n-tys, round toothpicks, pinholder straightener, fine spray, test tubes, clay, chicken wire, clear masking tape, pastel chalk, scissors, clippers, florist knife, hand cleaner, plumber's lead holder, pipe cleaners, florist picks, green thread, floral tape, tuck tape, ratwire, and wire. (Photo: William Sevecke)

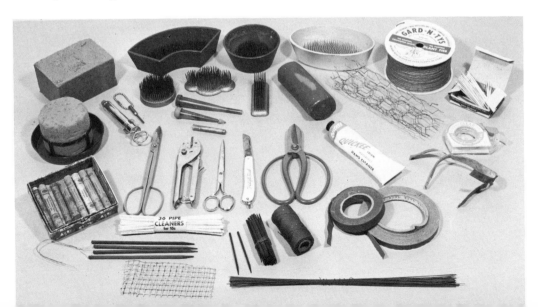

THE DECORATIVE UNIT

Oasis: a hydroscopic material that retains water after soaking; available at your florist in green blocks 6 x 3 x 12 inches. Cut to size with knife, soak several hours; drain; place in container or wire into shallow dish. For a candelabrum arrangement cover Oasis with aluminum foil. Oasis is expendable, but it is nevertheless a timesaver and very useful.

Styrofoam: (green or white) useful for fruit and vegetable arrangements, dried arrangements, and Christmas arrangements.

Additional aids: keep the following in your kit or basket: thumb tacks, straight pins, safety pins, hairpins, matches, tin foil, glue, pastels, and green florist thread.

ACCESSORIES

An accessory is something that aids the principal design or assists the main feature subordinately. It must be contributory, supplemental, or additional to serve as an accessory.

In table settings and flower arrangements accessories contribute to the design by emphasizing the color and/or accenting the spirit or mood. They may be used as a featured note for emphasis or for added interpretation. They must show relationship in color, texture, scale, and story to be in keeping. Their function is to enhance and to unify both the composition and the table setting. Unless the accessories contribute either to the design, color, or mood, they should not be used. Unrelated accessories destroy visual balance and spiritual harmony. Care should be taken not to use them just to fill space. In order for an accessory to be woven properly into a composition, it should be incorporated into the design when it is planned. It should not be an afterthought added without relation to size, color, balance, or meaning.

Compatible accessories can augment a limited amount of plant material to produce a happy result. However, when a large figurine or other large object is used as the predominant feature, it no longer serves to aid or supplement the composition. Therefore it is *not* an accessory. The figurine or object becomes the dominant interest, and the plant material becomes subordinate, aiding and enhancing the figurine or object.

CANDLES

Candles contribute greatly to the beauty of any table. Their soft glow spreads magical glamour not supplied by other types of lighting. Like the other accoutrements of your table, they must be considered for style, size, and color, so that they are pleasingly coordinated and become an integral part of the setting (see also Chapter 13).

Candles are an inexpensive though artful addition to your table. They can be used for formal and less formal occasions singly, in pairs, or in large groups with equal success.

Height and type of candles depend upon the size of the table and the importance of the occasion. At a seated dinner, avoid having the candle flame at eye level. Either above or below is more comfortable.

Although candles can be purchased in many colors, often we have difficulty in finding just the subtle shade we wish. Here are a few ways you can tint or color candles to your own specifications easily.

Pastels. Rub soft pastel chalk directly on your candle; wipe down with a piece of moist cloth or absorbent cotton.

Cosmetics. You can tint candles with cosmetics. Today lipsticks come in all shades, from orange through red to violet reds; eye shadow comes in green, blue, violet, and bronze. Blend discreetly.

Tintex. When you have a great many candles to color, make a Tintex bath; holding the wicks, dip the candles in the bath until they are the desired color.

Sprays. Candles can be sprayed almost any color, plus silver, gold, and bronze; when spraying, a light covering is more effective than a heavy, opaque coating.

CANDLES IN AN ARRANGEMENT

If your candles are short, or if you wish to raise tall candles to make them even taller, use hardware cloth. Wind a piece of hardware cloth securely around the base of the candle, allowing the required number of inches to extend beyond the base of the candle. This suggestion applies only to candles to be used in Styrofoam, Oasis, or in a pinholder, where the artificial extensions will be concealed.

Novel ideas for your candelabra are discussed in Chapter 10.

Artful Tricks

The skill of the flower arranger develops through practice. New ideas and new short cuts come to you as you work. Here are some suggestions that have worked well for me that you may find helpful.

HOW TO MAKE GRACEFUL CURVES

Wide leaves, such as dracaena, ti, and aspidistra, can be easily curved. Fold leaf from tip to center, roll in the palms of your hands. The warmth of your hands will help make the leaf curl. Or you can clip a clothespin in the roll to hold the leaf until ready to use.

To wire a leaf, place a heavy wire against the vein in the center back of the leaf. Cover it with tuck tape, masking tape, or Scotch tape. The leaf can now be bent, shaped, or rolled, as you desire.

Scotch broom can be made to curve by soaking it first in warm water, removing heavy short stems, winding firmly with green florist thread, from bottom to tip, then shaping. Soak again overnight.

Most branches can be made to curve gracefully after soaking. Hold branch horizontally, using both hands close together, with the thumbs on the underside, and bend branch easily until you have attained the desired shape. The warmth of your hands, gentle coaxing, and patience are all that are necessary.

HOW TO REINFORCE STEMS

A thin stem will hold more securely if slipped into a piece of thicker stem, such as gladiolus.

Small flowers, sweet peas, daisies, violets, freesia, are all easier to handle if tied in small bunches.

Weak stems can be supported by wiring a florist pick or straight twig close to the stem.

HOW TO CREATE A DOWNWARD THRUST

A downward thrust of leaf, branch, or flower can be created by using two twigs. Place a wire through the leaf or around the branch or flower to keep it from slipping, then tie two twigs, one to each side of the leaf, at right angles, and wire above, below, and around it securely.

HOW TO HOLD LEAVES TOGETHER

Staple iris, yucca, ti, or other leaves at the middle or bottom.

HOW TO KEEP FLOWER BUDS FROM OPENING TOO QUICKLY

Wrap the buds individually in florist wax paper tightly. Place in ice water in a cool place.

For tulips, touch the inside of the petals lightly with egg white or glue, press together, and wrap heads individually. Place in a can with ice cubes.

To keep flower stems erect, wrap the bunch tightly in damp newspaper and place in tall vase or pail in a cool place.

HOW TO ANCHOR GRAPES

Grapes can be anchored by winding wire around the stem and then catching or looping the wire under one or two of the top small branches, bringing wire down to stem, and attaching to a florist pick. The pick is then inserted into the holder, Oasis, or Styrofoam. Hairpins too are useful when you wish to fasten grapes or other small fruits in Styrofoam. The hairpins hold the stems securely.

HOW TO USE FLOWERS AND FRUIT TOGETHER

Place a mound of Oasis in center of a tall compote, low bowl, or other container. Crush chicken wire to fit into the edges of the compote over the Oasis. Arrange fruit or vegetables in pleasing color combinations, using a variety of forms and sizes. The wire cage supports the fruit and helps you create a more attractive contour, while still allowing your plant material to be in water. Secure fruit with florist picks into Oasis if necessary.

HOW TO SECURE HOLDERS

You can fix your holders in place in a number of ways. Paraffin is preferable for a crystal or silver container. Floral clay is best for wood, pottery, metal, and containers with uneven bottoms.

HOW TO WATERPROOF CONTAINERS

Alabaster or porous containers should be lined with melted paraffin.

HOW TO ANCHOR DRIFTWOOD

Driftwood, manzanita, and thick or hard stems should be anchored securely to create a permanent structural line, but are difficult to impale into holders. One way to accomplish this is to nail or screw them to a piece of plywood or a rustic plaque.

Another way is to wind a small piece of hardware cloth around the bottom of the stem, extending about one inch below the stem and sufficiently far up to support it. Impale into pinholder.

HOW TO TREAT MAGNOLIA LEAVES

Magnolia leaves and copper beech leaves can be (1) changed from their green color to a lovely bronze, and (2) prevented from becoming brittle, by placing the stems in a solution of two parts of water to one part of glycerin. After about ten days to two weeks in the solution, the leaves begin to change color. When they are the tone of bronze you prefer, remove from the solution. They may then be used in combination with fresh flowers in water or dried flowers without water. They are handsome for use in autumn arrangements.

Conditioning

Always condition your plant material before arranging. Conditioning makes it perky, and it lasts longer.

Garden material should be cut early in the morning or late in the day, not in the heat of the day. Carry a pail into the garden to hold your plant material. Recut stems under water to facilitate absorption.

1. Cut stems with a sharp tool (knife, preferably).

2. Remove foliage from lower portion of the stem to prevent bacteria from forming.

3. Soak flowers and foliage in deep water several hours or overnight, in a cool, dark place, away from drafts. Cut flowers do not like heat or drafts. It is also a good idea to keep flowers away from direct sunlight.

4. Fruit and vegetables should be wiped clean. Exception: grapes have bloom (frosty surface) which should not be removed because of its natural beauty.

5. Woody-stemmed plant material, such as chrysanthemums, lilacs, forsythia, magnolia, fruit branches, and shrubs, can be conditioned by crushing the lower three to four inches of the stem with a hammer. This allows the water to be absorbed more readily. Then proceed as in 2 and 3.

6. Dahlias and poppies may be conditioned either by plunging the stems in boiling water or by burning three or four inches of the lower stems. Carry a candle to the garden, sear the end of the stem, plunge it directly into a pail of water. Then proceed as in 3. When using boiling water or a candle, be sure to protect the blossoms and leaves from the steam or flame.

7. Foliage should be washed, then soaked in a tub of water for several hours. Some

leaves can remain overnight, but others, like begonias, may become waterlogged and therefore should remain in the water only a few hours. After soaking, place stems in a container of water.

8. To revive wilted (not dead or old) flowers, cut stems freshly, submerge them up to their heads in hot water, about 110 degrees, and allow them to remain until the water cools and they have revived. Wilted leaves will respond to the same treatment, but must be completely submerged. Most wilted flowers and leaves will react favorably to this treatment.

9. Polish leaves by crushing a piece of florist wax paper—it is softer than the usual kitchen wax paper—and wipe this over the leaves. It gives them a beautiful, soft, natural sheen, so much more attractive than grease or wax. Absorbent cotton also works very well, particularly for soft or tender leaves.

10. Using sharp scissors, trim leaves that are damaged, torn, or oversized, to improve their appearance. Follow the shape of the leaf, cutting carefully.

11. Commercial flower preservative may be added to the water of your flower arrangements. It makes them last longer, and the water will not need to be changed every day.

Facets of Fine Flower Arranging

Finally, when you make your flower arrangement, there are certain precepts that it is well to keep in mind. Here is a check list for your convenience. Your arrangement should have:
1. A well-developed, strong linear pattern.
2. Interesting voids or spaces, unequally distributed, to add interest and variety.
3. Good balance and equilibrium.
4. Focal interest.
5. Depth, a three-dimensional quality.
6. Textural and color harmony.
7. Over-all unity.

In addition, here are a few suggestions to help you create an arrangement that is both distinctive and beautiful:
1. Watch the height of your arrangement.
2. Watch the weight of your arrangement.
3. Show part of your container, particularly if you use a low bowl, plate, or plaque.
4. Do not crowd the container with too much plant material.
5. Use only accessories that are related in color, texture, and/or spirit.
6. Correlate your decorative composition with your appointments in color, texture, and spirit.

Chapter 9

MAKE YOUR OWN CONTAINERS

WHAT could be more exciting than creating something out of nothing? What more fun than converting old discards into useful artistic containers, and what is more satisfying than making new ones at small cost? It takes but little imagination and ingenuity, something we all have, plus the courage to develop an idea. Once you are aware of your desire to create new containers, you will be amazed at the many possibilities that lie along your path every day.

Look through your cupboards, the attic, cellar, and garage. Keep a fresh eye open for discarded articles you put aside years ago, for one reason or another. You may find a pewter pitcher, a papier-mâché box, an old lamp base, a perfume tray, or some pressed glass. They may look different to you today and be just right to complete or create a new container. Keep alert when out walking, shopping, or browsing around antique shops, auction rooms, and lumber or junk yards. You will be startled and delighted with what you find. Some of the items may evoke new ideas; others may help you develop an idea you already have. Don't be afraid to experiment; the results are rarely disastrous and are often satisfying and exciting. It is fun to invent new containers and to convert old ones.

Every time I prepare a lecture, I challenge myself to do something new, something I have not done before. Frequently, I create a new design or combine plant material in a new way. But often I find that making a new container starts a chain of new thoughts. If I had to do the same arrangement, in the same container, the same way, each time I lectured, exhibited, or made an arrangement even for my home, I would become completely frustrated—the stimulation of this creative art would be lost for me.

Beautiful and interesting containers are often expensive, and who can find or afford to buy a new one each time one exhibits or entertains? Creating new, refurbishing, or converting old containers is the most gratifying solution. Some I have made were evolved from the most unexpected things.

79

Original plaques designed and made by the Hirsches. (Photo: Fried-Louis)

Originate and Improvise

PLAQUES

Plaques can easily be made from wood, plastic, glass mirror, or marble at little cost. These are particularly useful when a related container cannot be found to blend with your table appointments.

Procedure. First, determine the size and shape of the plaque in relation to your table—approximately 18 to 20 inches for a 72-inch table, and 9 or 10 inches wide would be satisfying.

Next, on a piece of heavy paper, sketch out your design (oblong, round, oval, free-form, or any interesting but not too fancy shape). If working with wood, buy with care, being sure to select a piece of seasoned pine, maple, mahogany, or whatever your choice. Have your lumber sanded smooth to save time.

When buying your wood, be particular about the grain if you plan to stain it. If you plan to paint it, the grain is not important. Allow at least two inches more than your pattern if you wish a beveled edge. For a straight edge, the exact size is all you need.

Then, with a jig saw or band saw, cut out your design. For the beveled edge, tilt the table to a 45-degree angle or less. If you do not own either a jig saw or a band saw, your local lumber dealer will gladly cut it for you.

You are now ready to apply the finish. After you have sanded the edges, the top, and the bottom satin smooth, you may stain your plaque. Use any good commercial stain, following the manufacturer's directions. Finally, wax it with any good liquid or paste wax, but only after the stain has dried thoroughly. Repeated waxing improves the patina.

COMPOTES

That alabaster compote that you have yearned to own, but which has been out of reach because you could not find the one you had dreamed about or because when you found it the cost was prohibitive, can be pleasingly simulated in wood.

80

MAKE YOUR OWN CONTAINERS

I made a perfectly beautiful compote as follows. At the ten-cent store, I bought a small wooden chopping bowl about 9 or 10 inches in diameter. I then took an 11½-inch newel post (an old chair leg would have done very well) and two small squares of wood, one four inches and the other five. I sanded all of the pieces to silky smoothness and then fastened the two squares together with glue. With a long nail I attached them to the newel post, the squares forming the pedestal or base. The chopping bowl was secured to the top of the newel post with a long screw, and a little glue was applied before tightening the screw. Then I painted the whole with flat white paint. After it was thoroughly dry, I brushed it lightly and sparsely with gold paint. If I had used black or brown stain, it would have had a marbleized effect. My compote is not alabaster, but it certainly gives the feeling of alabaster and satisfies my purpose perfectly.

PEDESTAL CONTAINER

A make-believe marble pedestal was made in the same way as the compote. I used a part of a bannister (a turned post would do) about 12 inches high. I cut a round disc of wood about 5½ inches in diameter for the top and small square bases for the bottom. They were all carefully sanded and then attached with nails and screws. I countersunk the nail on top of the round disc and covered it with water putty for a smooth finish. I

SO MUCH FOR SO LITTLE Compotes—metal and pedestal containers you can make.

STUDY IN BLACK AND WHITE Black wood pedestal, black plastic mat, black and white Script china by Rosenthal, smoky goblet, and white rehearsal figures. Lily foliage, philodendron, hostatum, spathiphyllum, small green succulents, and green grapes evoke contrast and harmony. *Arranger: the author.* (Photo: La Crosse, Wisc., *Tribune*)

painted it with dull black paint (you may use shiny enamel, if you prefer). A cup pin-holder was secured with plasticine onto the round disc to hold the plant material.

METAL CONTAINERS

Interesting containers may be made from drain pipes, giving you charming fluted vases. A roofer sold me the copper drain pipe for one (galvanized iron, of course, may also be used). I purchased the size and length I wanted for the finished container plus a piece of copper to be soldered to close the bottom. That is all there is to it. Some drains are plain and some are corrugated in several shapes and sizes; you have your choice. To finish, rub it with fine steel wool to give it a hand-finished look. These may be made in pairs, or one large and one small to be used as a unit.

PLUMBER'S LEAD CONTAINERS

Plumber's lead is a good medium for making an artful free-form container. Any shape and any size is possible. It gives you so much latitude. My procedure is as follows.

Buy a piece of plumber's lead; have it cut to the desired size, allowing an additional two inches or more for a flange. Wearing heavy gloves, start shaping the lead, pushing it in at one point and folding it back at another, until you are satisfied with the result.

If the container is designed to hold water, it must be at least two inches deep. Squared or mitred corners must be soldered; soldering is not necessary for free-form shapes.

BRONZE AMETHYST PEDESTAL

A newel post, half of a barrel top, a few squares of wood for your base are all that are needed for this one. All the wood should be carefully sanded and assembled, as described on page 81, before painting. Paint with amethyst or violet bronzing powders dissolved in bronzing liquid. This finish produces an iridescent quality that is breathtaking.

COLUMNS

Two forty-ounce juice cans, with only the tops removed, are the basic materials. Fill the can that is to be used for the base of the column half full with pebbles. Stuff crushed newspaper in the remaining space to keep the pebbles from rattling. This weighted base gives the column stability. Solder both cans together.

Now the column is ready for finishing touches. Spread the surface thickly with multi-craftex or water putty; keep texture rough and uneven like tree bark. Allow to dry well.

ONE OF A KIND (Photo: William Sevecke)

Paint white, ivory, green, brown, or any color desired. For a special touch, brush lightly with liquid bronze or gilt.

If shorter columns are desired, use only one forty-ounce can. These columns may be used in pairs, two the same size, or in a group with one large and one small. They may be used at the ends of a dinner table or for a buffet table.

New from Old

Refurbish unattractive, nondescript bowls, old fixtures, liquor bottles, and the like. Odd decorative metal bases (silver-gilt) can be transformed into compotes and charming containers. New life can be brought to almost any container with simple basic lines. They can be rejuvenated by a change of color and/or texture. Flat paint, enamel, or bronzing powders are recommended.

Flat paint is most pleasing because its effect is soft and dull, and it dries quickly. Try it on old metal scales in copper, chartreuse, blue-green, white, or black, for use on an attractive terrace or dinette table. Enamel may be used if you wish a shiny, bright, hard finish.

Bronzing powders are available in many colors: Pompeian green, amethyst, blue, brass, and copper, to mention a few. These powders must be combined with bronzing liquid or banana oil and are then ready for use.

Stains, shoe polishes, and nail enamels can also vary the finish and change the outer appearance of containers. For example, a charming little container for a Sweet Sixteen or May Day birthday can be made by painting a champagne glass with frosted pink nail polish.

Textural effects can be obtained by using hard-setting clay, wood, putty, plaster, and Multicraftex. If you are an avant-gardist, try cinders or sand mixed with your paint.

NAUTICAL AND NICE

Wind heavy white rope around a large No. 2 can which is lightly covered with glue. For an interesting center decoration for a small table, a group of three small squat cans that are also rope-covered may be used. These make clever containers for outdoor or nautical tables on land or sea.

PLASTIC MAKES PERFECT

Cover cans, any size you desire, with Con-Tact. This self-adhesive vinyl comes in many colors and designs, also in wood and marble finishes. It is rugged and waterproof and can be purchased in department, hardware, and five- and ten-cent stores.

Cut to size, remove the adhesive lining, and wrap around the cans.

Unfinished, shabby wood can be covered to make satisfactory bases. For example, bases for alabaster or marble containers can be simulated by covering squares or rounds of wood with marbleized Con-Tact.

All cans used for water should be painted on the inside with aluminum paint to keep them from rusting.

Nature's Heirlooms

An interest in driftwood as an art form has grown increasingly over the past twenty-five or thirty years. Many homes, modern and traditional, include it as an accent or accessory in one of its varied forms and finishes. We see it in its natural state, semismooth, or completely finished, as "sculptured wood." The type and the finish one selects are determined only by one's likes and dislikes and by the use to which it is going to be put—either in one's home or in a flower show. All three types have their own characteristic appeal, and when used in an appropriate setting they create an outstanding note of interest.

Many summers ago, while canoeing on Raquette Lake in the Adirondacks, I became aware of the odd and rare shapes of the branches and roots of the tumbledown trees along the lakeside. I found fantasy and beauty in these forms, and their possibilities seemed endless. I gathered several pieces of driftwood from the edge of the lake and others from the bottom. This was the beginning of what proved to be ultimately a well of inspiration which served as a satisfying source of artistic expression.

Driftwood is found along the shores of many lakes and rivers; some may be washed up on the sands from the sea along the coast. All of mine I discovered in lake regions of the Adirondacks, Maine, and Canada. They are pieces, not of rare wood, but of pine, spruce, maple, birch, or cedar, characteristic of the environs.

The first and most important factor in finding unusual driftwood is to develop a seeing eye. I have picked up and rejected hundreds of pieces of wood before selecting one that I thought had interest and artistic possibilities. Seeing and then discriminating can make the difference between an ordinary and a highly distinctive collection.

After having found a choice piece of driftwood, the way to proceed is determined by where you intend to use it and for what purpose. Unfinished, in its original state, it can be used effectively in a camp or lodge or in a flower show calling for an arrangement in a naturalistic container. Semifinished merely means cleaned and sanded. It changes the wood from a rough, crude texture to one less so, making it acceptable for use in an informal setting, such as a ranch house or simple suburban cottage. Finished driftwood (sculptured wood) lends itself to more sophisticated or conventional settings.

NATURE'S HEIRLOOMS Fantastic forms. Driftwood uniquely devised and beautifully finished. From the author's extensive collection of sculptured wood. (Photo: Fried-Louis)

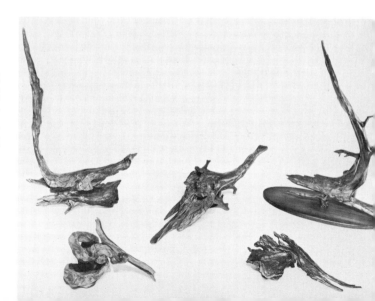

FORM AND FANTASY Natural driftwood container (antique finish), and smoothed weathered base are a foil for dracaena messangèana, velvet leaf anthurium, hen and chickens, limes, zucchini, grapes, tiny green bananas, and a pineapple top. *Arranger: the author.* (Photo: William Sevecke)

PROCEDURE FOR FINISHING DRIFTWOOD

Clean it first with a stiff brush. After the wood is thoroughly dry, sand it. Use coarse sandpaper to begin with, then medium, and if you wish a very smooth surface, finally use double-O sandpaper or emery cloth.

For the beautifully finished driftwood, which I call "sculptured wood," the previous

85

steps should be followed, giving careful attention to the final step, which is most essential for a fine finish. The sanding takes the most time but is worth it if you want a fluid, satiny effect.

Now decide on the color. Do you want it natural, walnut, mahogany, or maple? For example, to complement your table, you might choose red or brown mahogany; for your piano, walnut or pine, and so on. If you wish to use it mounted as an abstract piece of sculptured wood, you might leave it in the natural color.

Select a good oil stain, apply a thin coat, and wipe off after 15 minutes. Allow it to dry at least 24 hours. If you have time and patience, apply a second coat and again allow it to dry 24 to 48 hours.

Now you are ready to wax. Apply a very thin coat of liquid wax and rub vigorously. Apply a second or even a third coat for an elegant patina. This should give you as fine a finish as you have on most of the beautiful woods of your home.

The varied forms, finishes, textures, and colors are also adaptable to flower show work. But remember, in selecting nature's rare specimens, they must say something. They should have interesting shapes and a feeling of motion and flow. Lacking rhythm and interest, they are just static roots or stumps with no artistic value or appeal. In collecting woods, try to find pieces that have practical as well as artistic possibilities.

Sculptured wood can be compatible in any period home, it is so adaptable in design, color, and texture. Simple, unfinished pieces carry the spirit of the Early American homes; the more beautifully finished ones, the traditional; and certainly those that are dramatic in form complement our contemporary or modern homes.

What you discover in your adventures with nature's heirlooms will be an extension of your own imagination. We all see things differently. No matter. The only important thing is that we see.

Woodsy materials have an affinity for natural driftwood. The exotic and the more elegant plants and foliage are equally interesting and related if proper forms and textures are selected.

I have used almost every kind of flower, fresh and dried, wild and cultivated, and have always been able to find among my collection of nature's heirlooms some piece of driftwood that would be compatible and harmonious.

SINGULARLY EMPHATIC Pineapple, croton leaves, and blond sculptured wood make an effective centerpiece for an informal luncheon. Appointments: pandanus woven place mat, violet polished cotton napkin, cream-colored place plate, and amethyst soup bowl, tumbler, and cigarette accessories. *Arranger: the author.* (Photo: David L. Steindler)

Chapter 10

IMAGINATION PLUS

*I*MAGINATION is the spice of today's tempo, which stimulates us anew and brings freshness to our routine life.

No longer do we enjoy the stilted effect of the round bowl of crystal or silver stuffed with carnations or roses and asparagus fern, and placed in the center of the table, its stiff globular or fan-shaped design commanding much too much attention. Nor are we happy to sit down to our tables set with the same china, used in the same way, upon the same white cloth. It is devastatingly dreary. What monotony! It need not be so, if you will only open the door to the wide world of your imagination.

A little imagination can convert a monotonous setting into something novel and exciting. Even the simplest and plainest appointments need not deter you. All you need is the inspiration and the courage to be a little daring. Try to do something you have not done before; this will stir you out of your usual groove.

Imagination is the stamp of twentieth-century dining. Variety is vital. Co-ordination of appointments in texture, color, and spirit reflects fine taste, logic, and harmony. An unusual seating plan, an innovation in design or service exemplify some of the newer concepts in imaginative contemporary dining.

Styles and customs have changed. Rigid rules and certain conventions that controlled attitudes at the turn of the century no longer bind us any more. Now we set and decorate our tables freely, with imagination, guided only by our needs, desires, and artistic talents.

Rare and expensive appointments are no longer the hallmarks of a beautiful table. Cost is no barometer. Do not confuse rarity or cost of an object with its character. Good design and livability are the primary points in our selections today. Intrinsic value is no longer the only criterion. No matter how simple the appointments, a table can always have style. Good taste and good sense dictate what is fitting and satisfying today.

DARING AND DISTINGUISHED
The dainty tall glass container is lined with white paraffin. The outline material is a metal clothesline, fringed at the ends, entirely coated with clear glue, and sprinkled with crystal glitter. The delicate roses, also slightly dusted with crystal glitter, add elegance to this exquisite arrangement. *Arranger: Mrs. W. Harrell Wilson.* (Photo: Mills Steele)

Imaginative Flower Arrangements

An imaginative flower arrangement can play a major role in creating a beautiful and exciting table setting. It is one of the most versatile ways of elevating an otherwise plain or undistinguished setting. An arrangement need not be costly to be charming and smart.

Nature is indeed our helpmate. Her gifts are abundant and diverse, affording us endless sources of inspiration at little or no cost. It is important to become aware of the plant materials available in our environs at the different seasons and in their various stages from bud to seed to recognize their potentials. When we do, we are visually and artistically attuned to the beauties and possibilities of nature.

Flower arrangements that can be made quickly are a boon to those who have limited time but still feel the need for living beauty. Even the busiest housewife can make conversation pieces to delight her family and friends with little effort and in record time.

Here are a few ideas that should stimulate your imagination. Use them as springboards for your own creative efforts.

QUICKIES

Apple arrangement. On a flat wooden plaque, approximately 9 by 15 inches, place a 3-inch pinholder. Impale a large green apple, stem side down, onto the center of the holder. Select six flat leaves, two long and four shorter. Try rubber plant leaves, dracaena, croton, large magnolia, or any tailored leaves. Place three leaves on each side of the apple in the holder, with the longest leaf in the center and the two shorter ones overlapping on the sides. Arrange and attach smaller apples with toothpicks around the center apple. Cover the exposed portion of the holder with ivy leaves. Place small clusters of andromeda, pachysandra, or pittosporum where the leaves join the apples. If you wish to

SPRING SUNSET Dramatic accessories, sculptured wood container and bread tray, and terra cotta head contribute notes of distinction to this beautifully balanced and correlated buffet setting. For detailed description of arrangement, see the photograph on page 30. *Arranger: the author.* (Photo: William Sevecke)

INDIAN SUMMER The homespun tablecloth, Italian and Danish dinnerware in yellow, gold, and copper tones, free-form handmade salad bowl, and sleek copper skillet are attractively correlated accoutrements. Copper beech, pandanus, diffenbachia, and spider mums (in two tones, gold and bittersweet) are sensitively arranged in sculptured mahogany wood to complement and enhance this informal company buffet. (Functional buffet setting) *Arranger: the author.* (Photo: Richard Knapp)

elaborate a little, you can add a few small bunches of grapes. A group of rose hips, if available, add a distinctive touch (see Christmas variations, Chapter 11).

Vegetable arrangement. A charming arrangement can be made of garden or florist greens and can be achieved with a few tailored leaves, dracaena, ti, aspidistra, clivia, or amaryllis and two or three artichokes or green peppers.

Ornamental kale. Do you grow ornamental kale? You should, because it is beautiful and not too difficult to grow. Its ruffled, fine-textured leaves appear in an array of delightful color combinations: shades of mauve pink edged with green, chartreuse, and green are but a few of the more usual blends. It is suitable with most china and glassware, except the very refined or delicate.

This charming cousin of the cabbage may be used singly if it is large enough. Or two or three rosettes can be grouped together with little or nothing added to it. This makes a quick and lasting centerpiece that is most enchanting.

INFORMAL STUDY (DOWN TO EARTH) Rhubarb seed, rhubarb foliage, and grapes on a driftwood plank make a charming, quick, and low-cost arrangement. Appointments: pink woven straw mat, Italian pottery (pink, blue, violet), and green tumbler. *Arranger: the author.* (Photo: William Allen)

Leaves and vegetables arrangement. Try privet hedge, common in the North, or shiny ligustrum, native to the South, florist lemon leaves or huckleberry for a simple, inexpensive, and satisfying arrangement. They can be used either vertically or horizontally. Select graceful, slender branches for your structural outline. When using lemon leaves or privet, they often need a little help. Prune foliage where it overlaps to create voids and to improve the pattern. After establishing your design, reinforce the main line with several shorter lines of the same or other compatible foliage. At the point where the lines of your design converge, place a small head of savory cabbage with several of the outer leaves rolled back, or three artichokes. This creates your focal area. Select a container suitable for your setting and the plant material. A pinholder or Oasis, florist picks, and hairpins are the mechanical aids.

Buds and blossoms. Build a centerpiece of a few buds, half open, and fully open flowers in a Swedish glass celery dish, an oval vegetable bowl, or a silver bread tray. Keep the design free and the structural lines emphatic. Introduce foliage if it is needed to reinforce the main lines, to create depth, or to conceal the pinholder. Care should be taken not to use foliage as a filler, as it will detract from the feeling of space, the varied voids, and the perfection of the design. Be sure that a portion of the container is visible.

Flowering branches. Three lovely flowering or fruit branches with flowing lines and striking voids plus one, two, or three blossoms are charming on a breakfast table. A miniature version of this arrangement would be delightful on a TV or breakfast tray.

Potted plants. Unexpected guests and not a flower in sight! Use one of your potted plants—pothos, succulents, geraniums, begonias, whatever you have—to make a centerpiece in a jiffy!

Using galax or ivy leaves that have been conditioned, wire stems (leaving enough wire to support the back of the leaf), bend, then place the wired stem in soil. The leaf should hang down and hug the lower part of the pot, concealing it. A second row of leaves should overlap the first. If the pot is large, a third, shorter row can be added. Set it on a round or free-form base alone or you may discreetly incorporate figurines, candles, or fruit.

FLORAL CENTERPIECES FOR BIRTHDAYS, ANNIVERSARIES

Oasis cake. Place two tiers of Oasis, five inches and nine inches in diameter, one on top of the other; cover with pachysandra and pittosporum or boxwood. Decorate with poeticus, jonquils, sweetheart roses, and andromeda. For another version try candles in the top layer and arrange carnations and ribbon bows all around the exposed edge of the bottom layer.

Curtain rod rings. Figures hold a garland of light foliage and flowers. Scotch tape or masking tape will secure small brass curtain rings to figurines. Intertwine a previously-made garland into the rings, starting at each side and working toward the center figure. Small flowers may be placed in groups in the garland.

Hearts and flowers. This is an ingenious arrangement that may be used for Valentine's Day. Mount a red heart into Oasis in a compote. Let cycus palms, white snapdragons, and red carnations follow the contour of the heart, and finish with rosettes of pittosporum. Have red ribbons flowing down from the sides of the container onto the tablecloth.

ILLUSION Liriope, Peace roses, and white delphinium appear to be resting in space, but in reality are placed on a most unique crystal stand. Three pieces of plate glass (one 10 by 18 inches and two 5 by 18 inches) are held in place by a piece of wood slotted on four sides. A round disk is attached to the top of the wood. The flowers are arranged in a cup pinholder. *Arranger: the author.* (Photo: Globe Photos)

HOW TO CREATE NOVEL ARRANGEMENTS

As you continue to search for ways to develop your own novel ideas, remember that unfamiliar plant material frequently presents an original note. So does familiar plant material used in an unexpected fashion.

Containers not primarily meant for flowers can also add a distinctive touch. Try sculptured wood, a porcelain lamp base, or a silver revolving tureen. The change from the customary round bowl and the unimaginative bouquet design is sure to give your table its first real lift.

Another way to create novel ideas is to vary your containers. Take old containers, candlesticks, ten-cent store pottery and figurines and spray them with enamel, flat paint, or gilt. This is often an easy and inexpensive way to transform a dull, uninteresting table into a delightfully co-ordinated setting.

Candelabra Arrangements

Many years ago I designed one of the first candelabra floral centerpieces with fresh flowers. It was inspired by the need for an important centerpiece for a comparatively small round table. The 54-inch round table I had to decorate could not have taken both a flower arrangement, tea service, and candelabrum. The idea of embellishing a candelabrum to make a dramatic unit seemed to be a new and attractive way to create an effect and still keep the table uncluttered and in good balance.

Though the result of my first attempt was novel and appealing, there was one discouraging factor. A few hours after I had completed the arrangement, the plant material began to wilt sadly. I had used Styrofoam to hold my plant material. Even though the plant material was well-conditioned, I soon discovered how impractical this was. Since that time a new hydroscopic material called Oasis has been introduced into the market. It retains moisture and holds plant material quite successfully. It is available at most florists, and it comes in green rectangular blocks that may be cut with a knife to any desired shape and size. It is also available in three-inch rounds.

TO PREPARE OASIS FOR CANDELABRUM

1. Divide the block of Oasis into eighths. Soak three or four pieces, which should be sufficient for the average-sized candelabrum, in water for several hours. Remove from water and set aside to allow all excess water to drain. The Oasis now retains only the water it can hold, and there should be very little dripping.

2. Cover each piece of Oasis with either Pliofilm or aluminum foil, folding the edges over tightly. The Oasis is now ready to be attached to the candelabrum.

3. To be sure not to scratch or injure your candelabrum, particularly one of silver that you may value, cover long lengths of medium heavy wire with floral tape by winding carefully so that no wire is exposed. Or you might use the new "Gard-en-tys," which comes on a spool.

4. Attach the Oasis to the candelabrum, using this wire; secure it well so that it will support the weight of the flowers.

5. Establish your outline, either symmetrical or asymmetrical in design, with graceful branches, foliage, or slender flowers inserted in the Oasis. Create a three-dimensional effect by placing some plant material on both front and back of the candelabrum, even if

FROM ANTIQUITY TO THE PRESENT Antique china and a George III silver candelabrum are combined with present-day embroidered organdy doilies and fine crystal. Miniature variegated euonymus, variegated pittosporum, green grapes, tiny green bananas, and green orchids exquisitely embellish the candelabrum in this very contemporary arrangement. *Arranger: the author.* (Photo: William Sevecke)

CHARM AND DELICACY White lilacs, lilies of the valley, pink carnations, and bits of andromeda grace the silver candelabrum. Pale pink tablecloth with embroidered inserts, cut crystal, Apple Blossom china by Syracuse, and pale pink candles unify this setting in color, texture, and spirit. *Arranger: the author.* (Photo: La Crosse, Wisc., *Tribune*)

it is only to be viewed from one side. Develop the design with transitional material. Larger, stronger forms and/or color at the focal area tend to unify the design.

POPULARITY OF DECORATIVE CANDELABRA

Decorative candelabra have become very popular in the past few years. Their arrangements can be as varied in style as the candelabra themselves. You can run the gamut in design from the simplest to the most elaborate, and combinations can range from delicate flowers to fruits, pods, foliage, and vegetables.

Silver, crystal, gold (gilt), porcelain, and alabaster blend well with formal settings. Pewter, brass, copper, heavy glass, wood, wrought iron, tin, and majolica are appropriate for less-formal settings.

As decorative units, floral candelabra can grace either tea tables, buffet tables, or seated dining tables.

As novel centerpieces, candelabra arrangements are a new adventure in flower arranging for table settings. They can be unusual and impressive, and they are expedient.

NOVEL AND ELEGANT Old Sheffield silver candelabrum is designed for a festive occasion—nostalgic colors, delicate textures, and sculptural quality suggest style and elegance. Apple blossoms, lilacs, pale pink carnations, pittosporum. *Arranger: the author.* (Photo: William Sevecke)

95

Fresh Plant Material

There is nothing quite like fresh plant material to enhance your dining table. Its beauty, diversity, and flexibility are most appealing. The freshness, fragrance, and vitality are attributes that neither dried nor artificial material can boast of. (There are exceptions: when other than fresh material may be appropriate or even more descriptive in interpreting Thanksgiving, Christmas, winter, and seaside settings. For these tables dried wheat, corn, pods, flowers, foliage, and even treated, painted, and artificial [for Christmas only] materials sometimes help to tell a story more effectively.)

Generally speaking, compositions of all dried or all artificial plant material are neither appropriate nor appealing for the dining table. As we work with fresh plant material we become aware of the endless varieties of colors, forms, textures, fragrances, and distinctive beauty.

Quantities of flowers alone do not necessarily contribute to a beautifully designed table. It is what we do with what we choose to use and how we organize it that makes it a conversation piece. Neither quantity nor cost produces beauty. A single blossom at the height of bloom, a flowering branch, some unusual foliage, a cluster of berries, seed pods, or a few buds can add that unique touch of originality to an otherwise stereotyped arrangement.

COOL BEAUTY OF GARDEN GREENS

The heat and humidity of the summer are no kinder to cut flowers than to us humans. They droop all too quickly, and their perkiness is rather short-lived.

Summertime is a time for relaxation, and arrangements that fade soon and have to be replaced frequently are not too appealing. Yet we love the presence of fresh plant material in our homes. It does something that neither dried nor artificial flowers can do. Its freshness, vitality, and fragrance give a lift to the simplest or most elaborately decorated home.

The solution may be fresh greens, either from the garden or the market. Use them alone or as a foundation accented with a few flowers, easily replaced. In the summer heat, cool greens look refreshing; they are crisp and perky and last much longer than most flowers.

During this season, focus your attention on your garden. Look for branches, shrubs, pods, succulents, foliage in rosettes, group formations, or individual leaves. You will find a galaxy of delightful plant material in your garden for your arranging. Appraise it for its form, color, and texture when gathering. Ask yourself: Does it have a clearly-defined linear structure? Will it serve as transition? Would it make an effective note of emphasis? Is its form plain and well defined, or is it fussy? Consider the color too. For even in greens you will find many subtle nuances: the fresh yellow greens; the clear bright greens; some striped or flecked with white; muted greens fused with haunting shades of violet, pink, or red; the blue greens and the lovely soft gray greens that go with almost everything.

Textures also reveal various qualities. You will find greens that are crisp, soft, glossy, lacy, velvety, leathery, satin smooth, or suèdelike.

If you think along these lines when gathering your garden greens, you will be able to organize your plant material with ease and speed into attractive, lasting designs, so appealing for hot summer days.

GARDEN GREENS YOU SHOULD KNOW AND GROW
The following are a few suggestions for your medium-sized arrangements:

Structural	*Transitional*	*Focal and Finishing*
aspidistra	aucuba	andromeda (Pieris japonica)
Burfordii holly	baptisia	apples
euonymus	canna	azalea
forsythia branches	castor bean	cabbage (small)
huckleberry	euphorbia	coleus
inkberry (Ilex glabra)	hosta (plantain lily)	galax
iris foliage	leucothoë	ivy
ligustrum	magnolia	mugho pine
lilac branches	pods:	pachysandra
lily foliage	baptisia	pears
pods (see *Transitional*)	hemerocallis	peppers
Scotch broom	lilies	saxifrage
tulip foliage	poppies	succulents (rosette types)
yucca	sedums	

Many of these greens are interchangeable. It depends largely on the size of the arrangement. For a small arrangement, leucothoë might be too heavy for the structural outline, but for a large arrangement it would serve well. Euonymus is adaptable as outline or transitional material, depending upon its fullness or slenderness. Aucuba could be used to reinforce a main line, and a rosette of it would add emphasis and create a center of interest.

Often structural material may be used as transitional material and vice versa. Some transitional material may be satisfactory for focal material, and can be reversed. But rarely can structural material or focal material pose for each other.

Chapter 11

ACCENT THE THEME

TABLE décor is comparable to stage settings in the theatre. A playwright does not think first of his scenery and stage setting, but rather of his theme, his characters, and that which he seeks to portray. So it is with table setting. We too should think first of the theme or occasion, then choose the appropriate appointments and seek to dramatize the setting to highlight the occasion.

As a playwright assembles the cast for his play, so we assemble our appointments, china, linen, crystal, silver, and floral arrangement for either a special or an everyday occasion.

In the theatre a dress rehearsal is in order. It is in order also, particularly for special occasions or flower show exhibitions, to plan and set our table in preparation for the event; not at the last moment, but sufficiently in advance to make changes if necessary. This rehearsal generally guarantees a smooth, more effective, and successful performance.

Themes and Occasions

A fascinating array of table settings can be created if you have a theme as an incentive every time. There are so many occasions, general and specific, that can provide stimulus. Just allow your imagination to roam.

Think of a summer brunch: cheerful colors and informality come to mind. A formal engagement party suggests elegance, candlelight, and festivity. A buffet supper might inspire you to try something dramatically different, while a barbecue would most certainly be practical and strike a note of gaiety and informality.

More specific events can set the theme for original and exciting tables. Think of all the holidays: Thanksgiving, Christmas, Easter, and Mother's Day, to name a few. Personal events like birthdays and anniversaries will always suggest themes.

Special occasions or international menus, too, can determine the theme, such as Italian,

SERENITY An Easter theme portrayed by rhythmically curved pussy willows, glowing candles, a Madonna, and the horizontal placement of calla lilies. *Arranger: Mary Kittel.* (Photo: Fort Worth Photo Lab.)

Chinese, or Hawaiian meals, shore dinner, clambake, spring salad luncheon, and others.

When the guests of honor for whom the particular party is planned have individual interests or hobbies, you can incorporate this idea in either the center decoration, the favors, the colors, or the appointments. Be sure, however, to use restraint and good taste in not overstating the theme.

Accenting the theme is fun. It takes only a bit of thought and advance planning to produce something individual and quite distinctive. Your success will depend largely on a little courage salted with imagination.

Thematic Variations on a Basic Setting

A well-co-ordinated basic setting can be appropriate for many themes and for many occasions.

Suppose we start with the basic essentials: a gold-colored, embroidered, Italian church-linen tablecloth; gold-banded china and gilt-edged crystal. Now let us compose a few variations by introducing changes in color, accessories, or the decorative composition.

DINING IN ELEGANT STYLE

Use a centerpiece of Burfordii holly, roses in hues from gold to copper, and small branches of croton leaves to complete the arrangement, which is placed on a gold column. Silver candelabra tie in with the flat silver, providing a needed note of relief or contrast.

GOLDEN GLOW A golden wedding anniversary. Gold Italian embroidered church linen, white and gold china, gold-banded crystal, and alabaster and gilt candlesticks are a foil for the gold column, which is crowned by gold and Orange Delight roses, Burfordii holly, and croton leaves. The soft green candles and the green in the arrangement are a refreshing contrast. *Arranger: the author.* (Photo: William Allen)

GOLDEN WEDDING

Build your decorative composition with values of gold or white with gold. Roses, gardenias, snapdragons, ranunculuses, lilacs, gerbera, and acacia are some of the flowers that are congenial in color, texture, and spirit. Alabaster or gold candlesticks with white candles touched with gilt and Dirilyte flatware complete the setting and tell the story. By all means, a sentimental corsage of lilies of the valley and golden orchids for the young bride would certainly accent this theme. (Another golden wedding variation is described under Specific Themes.)

CHRISTMAS DINNER

Using the same cloth, china, and crystal, and again using Dirilyte, we will accent the spirit of Christmas with color. On an oval mirror sprayed with gold, arrange berried holly and bright red carnations. The red accent is picked up in the candles, which are set in simple Danish brass candlesticks.

Each table reflects elegance, dignity, and impressiveness. Each, however, has a different flavor and depicts a different occasion while using the same basic equipment. With these appointments your table can reflect a past era or can accent the present. The result depends upon your accessories and your decorative composition.

A lush, opulent arrangement with charming, elegant old appointments would give the setting a classic or traditional feeling, while a dramatic arrangement augmented with exotic plant material and modern accessories would just as surely accent the present.

Here are two other variations, using the same basic accoutrements.

SOPHISTICATED MODERN

Try an arrangement of green and yellow dracaena messangiana, golden calla lilies, and pothos on a tortoise-shell tray. This would be smart and typically contemporary.

THANKSGIVING

A stunning composition for this occasion would be small fruits, such as lady apples, limes, kumquats, red and green grapes, and rose hips, combined with berried branches, small ornamental strawberry corn, and wisps of wheat flowing out of gold crystal and ormolu cornucopias. Crystal candlesticks and pale gold candles add glamour and finish to this setting.

Specific Themes

ANNIVERSARY TABLES

Paper, wood, tin, china, silver, gold, pearl, etc. are but a few anniversaries that stir the imagination. The trick is to recognize your theme and follow it through.

Let us suppose we want to develop an amusing and different setting for a first or paper anniversary. Remember that the key guests on this occasion will be young; therefore, a gay, informal table is in order. The paper anniversary calls for original treatment and novel ideas. It gives us much leeway to demonstrate our ingenuity and create a smart, practical, and economical setting.

Suppose we start with the table covering. Paper, of course, would be my selection, not necessarily the ready-made commercial type, but one that could easily be made and which would be far more unusual.

Papers come in rolls or sheets in solid colors or in attractive designs. Even kraft paper has possibilities. The width may be too narrow for your table, in which case seam two half-widths of the paper to either side of a central panel. Seal the seams with Scotch tape, or cover the seams with bands of ribbon or masking tape which may be used in compatible or contrasting colors. Appropriate, humorous sketches or clever sayings crayoned or drawn with Magic Marker onto your kraft paper can make it distinctive. Another idea is to superimpose motifs, flowers, and figures depicting hobbies of a personal nature. One might also appliqué paper or other materials in interesting colors and textures onto the paper table covering. The edges of the "cloth" may be scalloped or left straight. The drop should be short if the paper is stiff.

It is always fun to discover how one idea leads to another. You can use paper plates, cups, and napkins, or else you can use the many good-looking and serviceable plastic-coated appointments. They can be used as is, in color to blend with or complement your cloth or mats. If your cloth is a solid color, decorated appointments would add to the gaiety of the setting. You might even repeat your appliqué motifs on your cups!

A decorative composition of fresh plant material in related color would relieve the all-paper setting, making a refreshing contrast. However, if you feel you must carry your idea to the centerpiece, some paper accessories may be included. But *do* use some fresh leaves, flowers, fruits, or vegetables; otherwise the whole effect will be too stiff. This will give your table and arrangement a realistic and cordial effect.

In accenting the theme, it is not always necessary to have all the accoutrements match or repeat your idea in every detail. For example, it is perfectly acceptable, if you prefer, to use linen or cotton as a background for your paper appointments, accessories, and decorations. Often a suggestion or two is more subtle and much smarter.

This table setting describes a mood and accents the theme for a first anniversary party. It is attractive and practical. No laundry, no dishes, just loads of fun.

Paper settings of this kind, with variations, can be used for teen-age parties, business and professional luncheons, and church and civic organization suppers. Just be sure to associate or design some related or appropriate feature to accent your theme.

GOLDEN WEDDING ANNIVERSARY

For your background, choose yellow, gold, cream, white, or green in mats or table covering. Use your best crystal and china. Accent the theme with your flowers, favors, and accessories.

Old candlesticks, an old candelabrum, and old containers found in antique or thrift shops or even in your own attic may be sprayed gold. A bit of gold may be sprayed very lightly and unevenly on the lower part of the candles. Use gold ink for your place cards and gold paper and ribbon for your favors. The floral composition may vary from light to deep gold or may incorporate white if any of the other appointments are or include white. Emerald green or greens in several values can be used in small quantities for contrast.

PEARLS FOR JUNE

Pearls suggest the theme for a June birthday, for a thirtieth wedding anniversary, or a debutante collation. Through your container, accessories, place cards, favors, and flowers you can capture the lustrous opalescence of the pearl.

Cover an inexpensive or outmoded container or a pair of containers of glass or china with pearl-luster nail polish in white or pale pink. The effect is charming and delicate. Another idea is to use a large or several small conch shells or half shells with lustrous centers as your container.

Strings of novelty pearl beads may be used around the arrangement in garlands or may be incorporated in the centerpiece.

Pearl beads glued to your place cards and favors in attractive designs add to the theme.

Use flowers that are iridescent in color and delicate in texture, such as camellias, roses, freesia, triste, snapdragons, peonies, and ranunculuses.

The cloth may be white, pale pink, luster gray, or pinky beige. Candles, accessories, and flowers should blend harmoniously. A slight accent in color may be used, but the dominant over-all effect should be delicate and pastel.

THANKSGIVING FAMILY DINNER

Set the theme, selecting a large, pretty-shaped green squash or a gourd or pumpkin for your center decoration. Cut a slice off the bottom to level it. Cover the cut area with paraffin to protect it and keep it from spoiling. Hollow out a space large enough for a cup pinholder (or a can with a regular pinholder). Paraffin around the edges of the opening. For a cornucopia effect tilt your squash at an angle, then cut a slice from the bottom to make it rest securely, and proceed as above.

Make your arrangement of berried branches, wheat, oats, and chrysanthemums. Include seasonal fruits and vegetables, either at the base of the squash, which may be set on a wooden plaque or brass tray, or spilling out of the squash in profusion, symbolizing the bounty of the season. Kale or evergreens would make an attractive, timely finish.

HAPPY BIRTHDAY! Visually appetizing and almost good enough to eat, this "party cake" is easily made of seasonal garden material. The base is simply a piece of Oasis (approximately 6 inches round) lushly layered with inserts of pachysandra. The "frosting" decorations are andromeda blossoms, narcissi, and pink sweetheart roses. The beauty of the delicate centerpiece is enhanced by the antique silver tray. *Arranger: the author.* (Photo: William Sevecke)

THANKSGIVING SOUTHERN STYLE An imaginative use of exotic, nontypical materials for a Thanksgiving party—deftly organized around a spiral bunch of small green bananas are hearts of century plants, croton leaves, a pine bloom, pomegranates, chyotes, and grapes. The exhibitor wisely chose fruit and foliage in muted tones to complement the elaborate design of her antique lace tablecloth. *Arranger: Marie Johnson Fort.*

Earthenware, warm and gay in color, woven table covering, pewter candlesticks or molds, birds or barnyard figurines are but a few appointments that help us recapture the simple charm of our colonial forebears.

THANKSGIVING ACCENTS

Pecans, walnuts, and almonds can be made to simulate a bunch of grapes. They are ideal because of their lasting quality. The usual method of drilling holes through each nut in order to wire them together is both difficult and time-consuming. Here is a satisfactory short cut:

All you need is pieces of sheer nylon hose, cut in four- or five-inch squares, plus floral tape. Place a nut in the center of each square, tie it with wire, bringing both ends of the wire down about five inches, and cover the wire with brown or green floral tape. Then wind this taped wire around a pencil to create a coiling effect like tendrils. Attach a few fresh leaves to the bunch of "grapes." Try combining several bunches with just greens or two or three persimmons. Use them to accent your fruit or vegetable arrangement.

Christmas Ideas

Table Christmas trees have become very popular. They are easy to make and fun to construct by yourself or as a delightful family project. Large or small, tailored or fussy, they add a really festive note to your holiday table.

CONTEMPORARY CLASSIC A work of art is the focus of attention in this setting. The usual and the unusual in plant materials and accoutrements create a dramatic and rhythmic design against a tailored background. See decorative composition "Work of Art" on page 127 for details of floral arrangement. (Exhibition capsule setting) *Arranger: the author*. (Photo: William Allen)

SONG OF INDIA Voluptuous roses, in reds and yellows, and gray-green cedrus atlantica and rex begonia seem to sprout from the elegantly designed hollow brass-edged container. The lush cranberry linen cloth background is perfectly balanced by the delicate design on the Rosenthal china plate (Blush), the Swedish crystal goblet, and the golden ceramic bird. (Exhibition capsule setting) *Arranger: the author.* (Photo: Richard Knapp)

ALL AROUND THE CHRISTMAS TREE Choir boys chant around the table Christmas tree. Made of boxwood, the tree is hung with colorfully wrapped tiny packages, gold beads, bells, and butterflies. Real gifts are piled beneath the tree. *Arranger: the author.* (Photo: William Sevecke)

BASIC TECHNIQUE FOR MAKING CHRISTMAS TREES

Use any one of the following for your foundation:

1. *Cone-shaped Oasis.* This can be covered with green foil to give it greater stability. Soak and drain Oasis before covering it with foil.

2. *Chicken wire.* Cut a triangular piece and shape like a cone. Fill center tightly with soaked sphagnum moss.

3. *Styrofoam.* A two- or three-dimensional tree may be made by cutting three-inch Styrofoam in the shape of a tree or by buying a cone-shaped piece of Styrofoam. This base is particularly useful when using anything other than fresh plant material. Small pine cones, pods, and Hawaiian roses gilded and edged with glitter, or small Christmas balls with bows of tulle set in between them make charming and lasting Christmas trees.

DECORATION OR FINISH

An incredible amount of superb fresh plant material is available for these Christmas decorations. You may choose various yews, pittosporum, boxwood, ivy, galax, camellia foliage, or anything else that pleases you and is available locally.

Cut greens in short pieces, about three or four inches long. Soak several hours. Whittle the stems and place closely together into the tree frame (foundation). This is the background.

The tree can be set on a plaque, stand, or tray of any size or material you choose. It can be raised, if you prefer, by putting a long dowel into a block of wood (round or square and painted green) and by inserting it into the tree. This gives the tree a lift and a more natural look.

It can now be embellished in a whimsical, humorous, enchanting, or imaginative fashion to highlight your table.

DECORATIVE TOUCHES

The decorations on the tree can be geometrically or freely interspersed, or the entire tree may be covered with the following:

Brussels sprouts, lady apples, or crabapples. These may be placed on round toothpicks or small green florist picks and fastened into the tree foundation.

Cranberries, wired individually and then grouped in threes or fours, can be inserted at intervals around a larger tree. You may find long straight pins convenient for applying the cranberries singly on a small tree. For a complete cranberry tree, cover the entire tree closely. However, allow bits of green to show through to soften the contour.

Garland an all-green tree with ropes of iridescent beads or pearls. Hang a few angels, amusing toys, or velvet, satin, or tulle bows at random.

Small gift packages, glamorously wrapped, can be arranged at the base of the tree, ready for Christmas morning.

DELLA ROBBIA This adaptation is made of fresh fruits, gilded nuts, cones, pods, and taxus. It rests on a gold mirror and is flanked by gold and green rope candles. A lasting and effective centerpiece for a Christmas dinner table. Appointments: gold satin damask cloth, gold-banded service plates, St. Dunstan silver by Gorham, brilliantly cut crystal. *Arranger: the author.* (Photo: William Sevecke)

DELLA ROBBIA

Della Robbia is an adaptation of Della Robbia glazed ceramic sculpture developed by members of the Della Robbia family in fifteenth-century Florence. It depicted religious subjects surrounded by garlands of richly colored fruits and flowers on a blue background with touches of gold.

This elongated version I have found easy to use on an oval or rectangular table for a seated Christmas dinner:

Use Styrofoam as your foundation, covering it with any greens you desire. I have used taxus, boxwood, retinospora, or golden-tipped juniper successfully.

Select lady apples, crabapples, kumquats, lemons, limes, grapes, nuts, and gilt cones.

107

Wire individually with heavy wire. Paint or spray each piece with clear shellac. Invert and hook wire over wire hanger and allow to dry. Create your design on the greens by grouping the fruits and nuts and sticking them into the Styrofoam. Leave a space for the traditional bands of blue satin or gold metallic ribbon. Heavy green candles dripped with gold, placed at either end of the Della Robbia, make an excellent finish.

ALABASTER-LIKE FRUIT

Melt paraffin, add white lead or white paint a little at a time, or if you wish color add crayons or pastel chalk. Put heavy wire in fruit, dip in the paraffin mixture, and hang to dry.

FROSTED GRAPES

Frosted grapes are delightful to dress any table. Combine bunches of frosted grapes with holly to make a quick and attractive Christmas centerpiece.

Two or three bunches incorporated in a centerpiece of fruit add a festive touch.

Use frosted grapes to decorate a fresh fruit platter. They are delicious as well as picturesque.

Quick method for making frosted grapes. Beat the white of an egg lightly and add one tablespoon of water. Using a pastry brush, cover the bunches of grapes with the egg white, sprinkle with granulated sugar, and set aside to dry.

NUT CORSAGES

Using the nut-simulated grapes described under Thanksgiving Accents, here are two Christmas variations for their use:

1. Spray the nuts gold, then cover with sheer nylon squares. This gives them a soft old-gold appearance.

2. Spray the nylon-covered nuts with gilt, and sprinkle or touch with glitter for that Christmas sparkle.

Make a bouquet arrangement of carnations or red apples in a compote-type container, and surround the bouquet with gilt nut corsages extending over the edge of the container.

Use them also to decorate a fresh fruit arrangement or to supplement dried cones and pods which have been gilded, silvered, or sprayed white, to make a permanent holiday decoration.

For your lady guests, place a corsage at each setting and attach a place card. To have them serve a dual role, use them in your center decoration as described in the bouquet arrangement above. After dinner, you can present a corsage to each of the ladies.

CHRISTMAS QUICKIES

1. This is a variation of the quickie green apple arrangement described in Chapter 10. Use red apples and introduce evergreens. American holly or variegated holly (Ilex opaca) with its profuse red berries is particularly attractive. String cranberries on a long wire, then make a bow design; or place individual cranberries on short wires and group to-

gether to make clusters. Place either or both clusters and bow at the junction of the greens and the apples. In place of or in addition to the cranberries, green grapes may be used.

2. To transpose this arrangement into an even more festive one that captures the spirit of the season, Christmas balls may be used with the evergreens. Or your red apples can be made to sparkle like Christmas balls by spraying them with plastic or by dripping them with glue and dusting lightly with glitter. Ivy leaves that have been sprayed with gold or silver add a note of gaiety and a skillful and quite lasting finish.

HARK THE HERALD ANGELS SING This Christmas Eve buffet table is delightfully unconventional in its color scheme—the silvery green cloth with shiny threads is a lovely contrast for the brown napkins, California china in green, yellow, and brown, and the brown wood roll tray. Mugho pine, mahonia, and pine cones touched with gold are arranged enchantingly on a walnut plaque; the olive green rope candles and angels accent the theme. *Arranger: H. Hillman.* (Photo: Roche Photography)

Chapter 12

THE GOURMET TOUCH

By NOW we can see how far-reaching are the choices, yes, how interwoven are the elements of the art of table setting and gracious dining. Though we have not delved too deeply, we have emphasized the importance of good design, color harmony, trends, and etiquette.

Now let us discuss the relationship between our beautiful table and that fundamental element—food—so necessary to gracious dining. You can capture the spirit of any occasion by introducing a suitable menu that is integrated with its setting.

Our daily sustenance, which some of us in our hurried routine life think of only as satisfying hunger, is endowed with aesthetic properties. These we have mentioned throughout as color, texture, and spirit. This realization lends a whole new dimension to the magnificent art and grace of dining.

A beautifully co-ordinated table is further enhanced when delicious food directly complements the setting, when they seem to speak the same language. This tie-in quality admirably further accents the theme.

Visual Aspects of Gracious Dining

Most meals are planned without the stimulus of something extra special. Daily dining becomes somewhat routine. It would be unlikely that the same thought and attention would be given to detail in planning and co-ordinating all your everyday menus and settings.

However, if you have a feeling for design and an understanding of color, and if you give thought to special occasions, you will find that unconsciously you are doing the same thing from day to day.

Taste develops with practice. When things are right for each other, you sense it immediately; they seem to strike the right chord.

STRAWBERRIES AND GERANIUMS Fresh strawberries and geraniums accent the informal arrangement of berry-red geraniums with geranium foliage. Their brightness and freshness are enhanced by the dazzling white background and appointments. The gourmet touch (color-related first course) makes the setting gay and inviting. *Arranger: Christine Heineman.*

Alert and conscientious homemakers, like fashion designers, are always on the lookout for new ideas to give a fillip to everyday menus. There is nothing like a new twist to the usual menu to make people sit up and take notice.

Try your everyday foods in unusual combinations. Or introduce some unfamiliar foods and present them in a pretty and palatable manner. Such planned menus, co-ordinated to your table décor, will make any meal a delight. When menus are thoughtfully planned and the food is tasteful and visually delectable, you have achieved the height—the gourmet touch!

Plan your menu or plan your table; it does not matter which comes first. The same thought that you give to one must follow through to the other. It is not difficult to do so.

Color and spirit are the leveling factors that provide a good feeling, a feeling of belonging together.

A prettily set table and an unrelated menu, or vice versa, are only half the job. There-fore, it is important to correlate your *appointments, decorative unit,* and *menu* in *color, texture,* and *spirit* in order to achieve the ultimate in visual and gustatory dining pleasure.

The Danes have a saying, "Put flowers on your table before food." They have carried their love of flowers and color into their food. Their famous smörgåsbord tables are al-ways dramatic pictures. Even their smörgåsbord shops, which line the thoroughfares of Copenhagen, display delicacies, tray after tray of open sandwiches, colorfully designed and simply delectable. These are some examples of co-ordinated, superb artistry.

It is apparent that the Danes have known for years that beauty is important—beauty in everything. That is perhaps why they make such a fetish of the presentation of their food. They are gourmets enough to know that beautifully presented food gives double pleasure because it can be both aesthetically satisfying and palate-stirring.

Develop your menu with your equipment in mind. Menu planning and table setting are so closely related that it is difficult to think of one without the other. Certain foods require certain equipment. And certain foods are more palatable and pleasing when used with certain colors and appointments.

Examples: Bouillabaisse or *zuppa de pesca* requires soup dishes and perhaps a large soup tureen for serving. Macédoine de fruits must be served in a deep dessert dish, not on a plate suitable for pie. Casseroles, ramekins, and coupettes are required for other special foods in order to present them attractively.

Everyday appointments and simple foods that are co-ordinated can be as effective as the most elaborate gourmet menu with luxurious accoutrements. It is knowing what goes together that brings out the most in your food and setting.

Through the years we have come to associate certain foods and ideas, perhaps because of tradition or constant use. Corned beef and cabbage go hand-in-hand with hearty eating and an informal or Provincial setting. Can you imagine the following menu being served on gold-banded celadon china on a pale green damask cloth, with fine crystal and silver, enhanced by delicate pastel flowers arranged in a silver bowl?

Antipasto

Spaghetti and Meat Balls

Caesar Salad   Crusty Garlic Bread

Fruit   Cheese

Chianti

Of course not! Obviously, I have exaggerated the lack of co-ordination between the menu and the setting for the sake of emphasis. But you can easily see how inconsistent this would be. The menu itself is satisfying; so is the setting. But the two are incom-patible, thus taking something away from both the food and the setting.

112

Serve the above repast on a beige-and-burgundy woven plaid cloth, with burgundy-colored napkins, tan pottery plates and platters, a wooden bowl for salad, a straw bread-basket, and a wooden tray for cheese and crackers. Fruit can serve a dual purpose: as the decorative unit and as dessert. It can be arranged on either a straw mat or a wood plaque. It is easy to see that this is indeed a more compatible setting. Its color and spirit tend to dramatize the menu.

Experts agree that for an informal meal any table setting within reason can be considered correct if it goes with the menu.

Tables designed for a special occasion or around a theme frequently suggest the menu. Sometimes the menu suggests the setting. For example, it is easy to co-ordinate menus for a Chinese supper, an autumn barbecue, a New Year's Day eggnog party, or a luau luncheon.

Color adds zest. It is just as simple to plan your daily menus and settings so that one enhances and brings out the best in the other; there is nothing less appealing than sitting down to a vapid table and a colorless meal. Just as disturbing is too much variety in appointments, discordant colors, and unrelated foods.

I wonder how much you would enjoy this luncheon: halibut, mashed potatoes, creamed white onions, vanilla-frosted angel-food cake, served on a white cloth with clear crystal. It sounds as though everything goes together well. But this is a case of too much togetherness, too much sameness. Both the table and the menu lack excitement and variety. There is a dearth of contrast visually and palatably. And contrast is the virtue of a smart and delectable meal. It would certainly spark this luncheon and make it more appetizing and appealing.

It is so easy to add zest to this visually unattractive meal and setting. It cries for color. Change the vegetables from white to green by substituting either peas, wilted lettuce,

STATELY BEAUTY Sculptured and varied forms of artichokes, peppers, zucchini, mushrooms, fungus, and sansevieria are harmoniously organized in an original and beautifully executed composition—for terrace or informal entertaining. *Arranger: the author.* (Photo: *The New York Times*)

puréed spinach and mushrooms, baked zucchini, or water cress garnish. Or change the vegetables to red, with horseradish shoestring beets or baked tomatoes with basil. You could change them to yellow or orange by serving glazed carrots or squash. These are only a few simple variations that would give a lilt to this menu and setting.

Next, you could re-echo the newly chosen color in either your glassware, table covering, or flower arrangement. Now your table and your food begin to sing and your table comes alive.

As you can see, there is not much needed to improve the meal. Only a bit of thought, a little advance planning, and your menu and your setting acquire a vital and inviting look.

I know this seems exaggerated, but I fear it is not. Too many meals are planned without any thought of the visual appeal. And you know as well as I do that good food tastes better when it is attractively presented. That is why the gourmet touch is so important.

Epicurean Aspects of Gracious Dining

The gourmet touch is the quality that transforms mundane foods into epicurean delights, not only by superb cuisine, but also by artistry. Select foods that go together and emphasize each other. Be sure they are correlated in color, texture, and spirit to each other, to the appointments, and to the occasion.

Every meal should combine foods that have an affinity for each other, plus a note of contrast. They should appeal to both the eye and the palate.

Keep in mind the elements and principles of design already discussed in Chapter 5. They follow from your flower arrangement to your table setting, to your menu and your food.

Select your main course. Other courses should be keyed to the dominant course, foodwise and colorwise. For subtle emphasis, interest, and variety, your menu should include one or more of the following:

Something hot	Something cold
Something sweet	Something tart
Something crisp	Something soft
Something rich	Something plain
Something spicy	Something bland

First impressions are generally the most lasting. So it is with your dining table. Carefully stage your opening scene by selecting a first course that is suitably blended with your setting in color, or select one that will heighten it dramatically. A clashing first course can be a very disturbing note.

I would never serve tomato soup or shrimp tomato aspic for a first course if my table covering were a shocking pink or burgundy. A strong-color first course is more appetizing when served on less-intensely colored china and also with a table covering of subtle hue.

Another incongruous combination would be lasagne served on delicately flowered china set on a pale pink cloth (an actual case!).

Try to sustain the color interest through the meal and certainly echo it in your finale. The dessert itself or the color of the dessert dish or plate can easily emphasize your story.

MENUS AND SETTINGS MUST BE GOOD COMPANIONS

The gourmet quality is the quality that changes a prosaic meal into beautiful poetry. An ancient proverb says, "Customs and manners may differ, but the love of flowers is universal." Foods, like flowers, have universal appeal. But they must be selected, combined, and served with the gourmet touch. Even the most everyday foods can have the gourmet touch if they are tastily prepared and visually aesthetic.

Delicious food attains the height of culinary art when presented in a well-correlated setting, highlighted by a beautiful flower arrangement. This combination is the ultimate in gracious dining. Gracious dining does not necessarily mean lavish, expensive appointments and rare, exotic foods. The feeling of hospitality comes from a desire for beauty and thoughtful planning.

The simplest dinner can radiate that beauty and warmth, transforming it into the quintessence of pleasurable dining.

Some of my pet menus and companion settings follow, for your inspiration.

TANTALIZING AND COLORFUL Luscious fruits and unusual succulents make a gay and appealing centerpiece for late summer or early fall. The range of colors and textures allows the hostess a wide choice in planning her menu and in correlating her first course. Arrangement: green bananas, red and Queen Anne cherries, limes, young green apples, and succulents. *Arranger: the author.* (Photo: Michael G. Spoto)

Compatible Menus and Settings

Appointments	*Decorative Unit*	*Menu*
Green Belgian linen Traditional floral china, violet and amethyst (Wedgwood, Purple Old Vine) Low amethyst goblet Silver (Tiffany's Provence) *Colors:* Green, violet, and amethyst	Colorful fruit arrangement: lady apples, prickly pears, plums, Tokay and blue grapes, and bits of andromeda, on driftwood	Cranberry juice Roast lamb Mint sauce Rosebud beets Horseradish Stuffed baked potatoes Blueberry tart Coffee
Blue and green woven mats Italian pottery, bold design in blue, green, chartreuse on white Stainless steel flatware Heavy green tumbler *Colors:* Blue-green, chartreuse, and white	All green arrangement of vegetables and foliage on a free-form wooden plaque, tray, or bamboo raft (zucchini, artichokes, peppers, okra, pachysandra, galax, philodendron)	Fish Tetrazzini Asparagus and pimiento salad Pecan muffins Baba ring, filled with fresh fruit Coffee
Ecru satin damask Lenox Wheat china or Rosenthal Stardust china Traditional sterling flatware (Gorham's St. Dunstan) Gold-banded tall crystal *Colors:* Ecru, gold, red	Silver revolving tureen, Red Happiness roses, freesias, camellia foliage Silver candlesticks, ivory candles	Crabmeat in avocado Petite Marmite Cornish Hen à la Bourbon, wild rice dressing Brandied peaches Green beans epicure Coffee royal parfait, crème de cacao Demitasse
Pink Alençon lace cloth Rosenthal Blush china or Syracuse Apple Blossom china	Pale pink lusters (pair) Low three-branch candelabrum Pale pink candles	Brook trout, shrimp sauce, water cress garnish Squab cerise Corn puffs

Pink frosted goblet
Danish sterling flatware
  (Jensen's Acorn pattern)
Colors: Pinks, pastels

Delicate arrangement of pastel flowers, trailing vines, in the rococo manner

Asparagus polonaise
Fraises Romanoff
Pink sparkling wine

Pale sapphire-blue linen damask cloth
Cobalt-blue gold-edged china
Dirilyte flatware
Hand-cut crystal
Colors: Blues, gold, tangerine, green

Arrangement of Talisman or Orange Delight roses, Burfordii holly and gerbera on a French gilt candelabrum
  or
Tangerine carnations and mignonette, Chinese holly, ilex, rotunda flora

Broiled grapefruit, ginger and kumquats
Soup julienne
Duck à l'orange
Glazed turnip balls
Orange-pineapple chiffon pie
Coffee diable

Amethyst-embroidered gray linen and organdy
Gray platinum-banded china
Platinum-banded crystal
Jensen's Acanthus silver
Waterford Lismore
Colors: Gray, amethyst, lavender, violet, violet-red

Squat candle centered on a silver tray or frosted glass mat, elevated on a small-footed stand; Better Times roses, single lavender stock, amethyst carnations (violet or blue grapes) euonymus
  or
Lavender fuigi mums, Better Times roses, aralia foliage

Honey balls in wine
Green turtle soup
Filet de boeuf
Spinach ring, mushrooms
Endive salad with artichoke hearts
Black cherries Jubilee
Dainty cookies
Coffee

Tomato-red, blue-green, and white plaid cloth
White pottery (modern)
  or
Heavy china
Tumblers, green or clear
Straw-handled cutlery
Colors: Red, blue-green, white

Arrangement of edible fruit: apples, pears, peaches, figs, oranges, grapes, pachysandra, on white pottery plate raised over a small inverted pottery bowl (serves as both dessert and decoration)

Spaghetti, garnet tomato sauce, richly seasoned with Italian sausage
Mixed greens, anchovy
Crusty Italian bread
Fruit (from arrangement)
Cheese
Chianti
Espresso

Buffet

Gold Italian church linen cloth
Green-banded china
    or
Rosenthal Sunburst
Gold-throated goblet
Dirilyte flatware
Colors: Gold, white, green, red-orange

Dramatically tall arrangement of forsythia, red-orange peony tulips, croton and aralia leaves, on a gold column
Accessories: Venetian long-tailed birds reflect the gold and repeat the red-orange in the flowers
Four brass candlesticks, celadon green candles

Coquille St. Jacques
Chicken marmalade
Glazed corned beef, spiced apricots, and apples
Squash ring
Peas and water chestnuts
Avocado grapefruit salad
Coconut snow balls (vanilla ice cream and orange sherbet)
Mandarin oranges, curaçao sauce
Coffee

Luncheon

Brown serge mats
Nils, Denmark (two-tone green)
Low-stemmed amber glassware
Tuttle sterling—Onslow
Colors: Brown, yellow, persimmon, green

Arrangement in natural driftwood container: pussy willows, spring flowers, fruits in shades of yellow and green accented with persimmon

Curried crab soup
Chef's salad: ham, chicken, cheese, deviled eggs, water cress
Sesame rolls
Deep dish apple pie
Coffee

Buffet

Black-and-white denim tablecloth
Black-and-white Wedgwood college plates
Swedish smoked crystal
Black wood-handled stainless cutlery
Stainless steel trays, bowls, platters
Colors: Black and white, orange-red

Valeria gladioli (orange-red), anthurium, large pothos foliage and orange-red anthurium, black container
Pewter candlesticks, gray candles

Bouillabaisse
French bread
Tossed salad, artichokes and tomato wedges
Raspberry and orange sherbet, framboise
Coffee

These compatible settings and menus may be used to tip the scales of your imagination. They are co-ordinated visually and gustatorially to suggest elegance or casualness rather than specific formality.

118

Part Three

Chapter 13

THE CHALLENGE OF EXHIBITING

Success is rarely accidental. Usually
it is the result of careful planning,
courage, and dogged persistence in
making the plan work.

A. R. BRADLEY

THIS chapter is written primarily for flower show exhibitors and judges or anyone interested in competitive exhibitions of table settings and flower arrangements. While lecturing and teaching in different parts of the country, I have been bombarded with questions *re* "Judging Dining Tables for Flower Shows." After many flower shows and at Judges' Council meetings, numerous questions arose concerning the tables exhibited versus the meaning of the schedules and their ultimate interpretations.

Exhibitors and judges alike have urged me to touch upon several points which have caused some concern and no little confusion. Though these may have been technicalities, and minor in some instances, they have taken on mammoth proportions.

In an effort to be conscientious and conform to the set rules, some judges tend to be too literal, often overlooking the beauty and message of the over-all composition.

The exhibitor in some cases penalizes herself by not studying and adhering to her assignment—the schedule, the law of the show.

The Attributes of Good Sportsmanship

Good sportsmanship involves honest rivalry, courtesy, consideration for others, diplomacy, and grace to accept the decisions, whatever they may be. For often we learn more from our mistakes than we do from our successes. Good sportsmanship is an admirable and essential quality which allows us to accept defeat and even success with graciousness and understanding. Many of these attributes apply to exhibitors and judges alike. Good sportsmanship is a quality that is needed to enjoy the competition of flower shows and to face all the challenges of life more easily.

Flower Show Tables

Table settings, one of the most popular classes in flower shows today, attract the attention of ever greater numbers; yet frequently they leave something to be desired from the point of view of practical table décor and superior artistic presentation.

We need not search too far for some of the reasons for this lack. The same person who misses out at a flower show might not make the same mistakes at home. She would never set a table without napkins (see page 141). Nor would she use her most elegant china and crystal on an ordinary crumpled cotton cloth. She would never plan her decorative unit so large as to overcrowd the table, knowing it would hinder all possibility of pleasant intimate conversation. These and other errors of omission and commission might occur or be overlooked on an exhibition table. I have seen these very things happen.

A flower show table requires much advance thought and planning, also a great deal of stamina. Real physical effort must be exerted in organizing and transporting every detail of equipment to the exhibition hall so that all arrive at the show in prime condition.

You would assume that the elements that contribute to a beautiful table for your home are the same as those for prize-winning flower show tables. Basically, they are. However, there are some respects in which they differ, and these differences must be recognized before success can be achieved in either.

At home a table and its setting are a segment of a completely related unit: your room, your home, your way of life. Your table setting depends on its surrounding décor—the wallpaper, the furnishings, accessories, and lighting, plus your table appointments—for an over-all harmonious effect (see Chapter 1). The established spirit, color, style, and size of the dining room are always present and are your gauge in setting your table. You are limited and spurred only by your imagination, talent, equipment, and the occasion for which the table is being planned. This well-defined area, the dining room with its related background and accessories, enhances the table setting. The table setting in turn becomes part of the whole co-ordinated picture, which should and does reflect your personality and your way of living.

In contrast, dining tables for flower shows are inspired and confined by several circumscribed necessities.

Facts Every Exhibitor Must Face

1. *Schedule:* indicates the theme, classes, rules, and regulations.
2. *Class:* states specific requirements, *i.e.,* interpretation, occasion, formality, and exact number of place settings.
3. *Staging:* describes placement, which may be an open area, a vignette, or room setting with wallpaper, bamboo, or painted screens.

4. *Table:* suggests size, type of table covering, and decorative unit.

5. *Lighting:* amount and kind determines the colors you might select.

6. *Competition:* adds excitement, causes some tensions, but nevertheless is a stimulating and valuable experience.

These requisites and limitations mean that more than the average amount of imagination, precision, and expert craftsmanship is needed to achieve recognition at flower shows. Unlike tables set for our homes, flower show tables generally have neither the correlated background nor the proper lighting to set them off. In most instances, your table will be one of a group of tables, frequently staged in unrelated and sometimes discordant settings. It cannot and does not depend on background décor for any aid. Therefore, an exhibition flower show table must be a complete entity and must tell its story so expertly as to be appreciated by connoisseurs and public alike.

It is not enough that your table's design is pleasing, that its colors and textures are nicely related, and that all the equipment seems to speak the same language. This most surely would present a pleasant table. But a prize-winning flower show table must do more than evoke a pleasant feeling. It must have that added quality which sets it apart. Such quality is exciting. It demands and holds the viewer's attention. It says, "I am different, I am superior, I am outstanding—I am smart." This extra vibrant quality of which I speak is known as *distinction.* Without it a flower show table rarely reaches prize-winning heights. How to achieve this quality is discussed further on.

CLASS: "MR. BACHELOR ENTERTAINS" Dignity and warm hospitality are reflected in this informal dinner table, with no extraneous fuss and frills. Appointments: black straw mats, white and brown pottery, violet napkins, black wrought-iron candlesticks, copper champagne bucket. Arrangements: champagne bottle tied with violet napkin and draped with purple grapes; Danish steak board holds an arrangement of eggplant, zucchini, yellow squash, violet and violet-red zinnias, lavender thistle, and purple grapes. *Arranger: the author.* (Photo: William Allen)

Your Exhibit: From Data to Deadline

The following reminders and suggestions serve as aids for those exhibitors who enjoy competition and are stimulated by creating flower show tables of beauty and distinction.

1. Your schedule is the law of the show. Read it through thoroughly; make a mental note of the theme and the class you wish to enter.

2. Reread your specific class, which may be by choice or invitation, competitive or non-competitive. Do you understand what is asked for? If you have any doubt, check with the consultant or the proper chairman.

3. Check the rules and regulations, noting the requirements and limitations of your special class (size of table, number of place settings, type and style of table, background if any, interpretation, and particular occasion).

4. Now relax and allow your ideas to develop. The theme of the show and the class should spark your imagination and start you thinking.

5. Send your entry in early, certainly before the deadline date, so as not to be disappointed. In large flower shows, request an alternate class should your first choice be already filled. This saves time, effort, and unnecessary correspondence for both you and the entry chairman. It also saves you the time and thought of planning a table for a class that is already filled.

6. Before assembling your material, write on a large sheet of paper the *theme,* your *specific class,* the *rules and regulations* governing it. Keep this before you and refer to it while working. It is difficult enough to win ribbons in keen competition; that is why it is wise not to penalize yourself by failing to adhere to the schedule rules. Rules are necessary in competitive exhibiting. They are a guide to the exhibitor and an aid to fair judging. Adherence to the schedule will eliminate the possibility of losing unnecessary points in judging, particularly in the following categories in the scale of points, frequently designated as:

A. Conformity to schedule; suitability to occasion or interpretation.
B. Compatibility of all materials.
C. Condition and fastidiousness.
D. Design (emphasis on scale, proportion, and balance).

Other categories found in the scale of points for table décor are Distinction and Originality, Functionalism, Perfection of Centerpiece, and the more subtle principles of Design (rhythm, dominance, and contrast). These categories demand creativeness and skillful craftsmanship, which vary with the talents and imagination of each exhibitor. Points under these headings cannot be prejudged. However, it is within the reach of every exhibitor to acquire the maximum or near-maximum number of points allowed in the scale of points for A, B, C, and the portion of D mentioned. This can be assured by referring to and closely fulfilling the schedule requirements.

7. Begin early to assemble your appointments (linens, china, crystal, container, and accessories). If you can arrange more than one setup, this will give you an opportunity to enter the one that is best correlated. Always check back to your schedule and notes to help you decide which appointments interpret your class most effectively. In table setting, appointments are generally chosen and organized before the plant material. This is because it is somewhat more difficult to acquire and co-ordinate the proper china, linens, and crystal than to find appropriate and related plant material. However, the reverse is possible, though not usual. The china, linen, accessory, theme, occasion, or plant material are but a few sources of inspiration. It is important to have a starting point, and anything that gives you that is a good beginning.

Follow your inspiration, originated by the schedule, select your appointments with an eye to *color, texture,* and *spirit,* so that the over-all effect is compatible and harmonious.

Scale of Points

Take careful note of the items specified under each category, because success depends upon careful advance preparation.

CONFORMITY TO SCHEDULE, SUITABILITY TO OCCASION, INTERPRETATION
1. Type of table to be set (breakfast, luncheon, dinner, tea, seated or buffet).
2. Style of table and degree of formality.
3. Exact number of place settings and/or required appointments.
4. Occasion or theme, accented by selecting colors, appointments, and/or accessories to best interpret assignment.

COMPATIBILITY OF ALL MATERIALS
Colors, textures, qualities, and spirit of all accoutrements need not be identical, but should be logical, visually and practically.

CONDITION AND FASTIDIOUSNESS
This category refers to both appointments and plant material. It is a requisite at all times whether you plan a simple or an elaborate table. Your linens must be not only spotless, but crisp. If you use a tablecloth, one center fold lengthwise is the most meticulous presentation. Wrinkles and unnecessary creases detract from the over-all crispness. Ideally, the overhang should be even all around. Your crystal should be sparkling and the china gleaming. Plant material must be turgid, fresh, and clean, with no residue of insecticides, no eaten or wilting flowers. Plant material with unpleasant or offensive odors should never be used. Use only flowers that will remain fresh throughout the show. It is the obligation of the exhibitor to keep her plant material in prime condition.

Flat silver has not been mentioned because it is not generally used for flower show exhibitions. Committees cannot be responsible for its care. Should silver be permitted, as in a Home and Garden Show, it should be bright and shining.

When using mats or doilies, they should be placed evenly at the edge or one-half inch from the edge of the table. (Exception: large round doilies may hang over the edge a little, but not so far as to interfere with the guest's comfort.) The spaces between settings should be identical, and the placement of the appointments on each mat or at each setting should be repeated with exactness. Napkins, folded evenly, should be placed in the same position at each place. Carelessly placed appointments detract from a neat, smart appearance. Their lack of precision can also disturb the balance and over-all unity of the design of an otherwise beautiful table.

OVER-ALL DESIGN

Each principle of design can be directly applied to table décor. This is discussed in detail in Chapter 5. Be sure that your appointments and accessories are in good scale and good proportion to the size of the table and in relation to each other and to the decorative unit.

Example 1. A very small centerpiece on a large table or a large decorative unit on a small table are both out of scale and out of proportion.

Generally, a good ratio for the over-all centerpiece, which may include candles, is approximately 20 to 24 inches long for a six-foot table. In other words, the area of the decorative composition should be about one-third the length of the table. The height of the unit must not interfere with easy cross-conversation and vision, nor should it be too massed. Approximately 15 to 18 inches is a good guide for a light and airy arrangement. For a small dinner party an even lower arrangement is preferable.

Example 2. A tablecloth having only a four-inch overhang for either a seated dinner or buffet would lack good proportion. An approximate overhang of 12 to 15 to 18 inches all around is a graceful proportion, depending upon the size and type of the table. For Victorian-type tables, tea tables, wedding tables, and some exhibition tables, however, the cloths may hang dramatically long, sometimes even just skirting the floor.

PERFECTION OF CENTERPIECE

The qualities to look for are described under Judging the Centerpiece in Chapter 14.

DISTINCTION

Distinction is a vibrant, striking, conductive quality. It is a quality which is often difficult to describe, besides being one of the most controversial points in judging. It is the offspring of both inspiration and technique. Without distinction an arrangement never quite reaches the height of artistic accomplishment in our contemporary style of table setting and flower arranging.

What is distinction? How do we know it? What do we mean when we say a table setting or flower arrangement has distinction?

Distinction is a quality of difference. It sets one thing apart from another by some distinguishing characteristics. In other words, an exhibit is distinctive when it (1) clearly stands apart, is outstanding; (2) has a distinguishing mark of quality; (3) is decidedly

WORK OF ART Bold forms, unusual colors, rare and common plant materials are skillfully wrought into a compelling and dramatic design. Sansevieria, staghorn fern (Platycerium), pothos, red anthurium, and a violet-red banana blossom heighten the rhythmic grace of the goddess of love and beauty, Aphrodite. See also color plate facing page 104. *Arranger: the author.* (Photo: William Allen)

CLASS: "A CONTEMPORARY LUNCHEON TABLE INTRODUCING A FOREIGN MOTIF" Twentieth-century appointments in black and white are repeated in this breathtaking arrangement: white tulips, variegated funkia, and a black-painted driftwood branch create an emphatic design of rhythmic beauty, restraint, and simplicity with a flair in the Japanese style. *Arranger: Mary E. Thompson.* (Photo: Skvirsky)

different; and (4) is superior. How are these qualities of distinction achieved? By using, employing, or introducing the following:

1. Unusual but related plant material, appointments, and accessories.
2. Unusual but pleasing color harmonies.
3. Clever use of usual, easily available plant material.
4. Smart blending of familiar colors or color harmonies.
5. An original idea or presentation.
6. An inspirational quality or message.
7. Superior craftsmanship, technique; a professional touch.
8. Simplicity, elegance, restraint, and dignity.

The selection of the unusual in appointments, color scheme, placement, accessories, decorative unit, or skillful technique adds that distinguishing touch. To illustrate, the appointments may include a lovely sheer white linen cloth with Belgian lace inserts over a pale blue or amethyst under cloth, a beautiful heirloom tureen, old hurricane lamps, rare Sèvres compotes, a stunning vermeil candelabrum, or an ormolu epergne. Your color scheme may be boldly dramatic, unconventional, subtle, or sentimental. Your seating arrangement and decorative unit may be unorthodox, provided the over-all setting is in good balance and practical. Exquisite traditional or cleverly interpretative modern or primitive accessories, a decorative composition incorporating some rare or unfamiliar plant material or presenting a new idea in its design, all contribute a note of distinction, as does the masterful handling of the simplest or most commonplace material.

How to Achieve Specific Effects

SIMPLICITY
Well-defined linear design; limited material; restraint in the use of color; uncluttered look in appointments and plant material.

DRAMA
Sharp contrasts; bold forms; unexpected color combinations; uneven, dramatic voids; overhead spotlighting; unusual placement of accoutrements and decorative unit.

CHARM
Softness in textures; softness in colors; choice of color harmonies with emotional appeal; easy transition; soft lighting.

ELEGANCE
Luxurious textures; opulent colors; exquisite, lavish appointments; candlelight.

GAIETY
Sunshine colors; light airiness; novel touches.

UP-TO-THE-MINUTE SMARTNESS
Distinctive, new equipment, used with restraint, sophisticated but harmonious striking color ensembles; avant-garde designs; unexpected combinations; emphasis on space integration.

COOLNESS ON A SUMMER DAY
Crisp salads, frosty beverages, straw mats, cool colors (white, green, pale blue), and glass appointments sparkling like ice are pleasant to the touch and vision on a hot day.

129

Points of Importance

FORMALITY IN FLOWER SHOW TABLES

Formality is an adherence to established rules and forms. Informality is a deviation from and a lack of conformity to established rules and customs. Both extremes and the many degrees between the two generally refer to *types of service* (see Chapter 7).

Formal occasions demand a number of servants for precise and proper service, while informal meals are often planned just as carefully but for casual service or without assistance.

It is not possible, of course, in a flower show to indicate the degree of formality of a table by the accompanying servants and service. The exhibitor has but one way she can portray the degree of formality of the table she sets. That is through the selection of appointments, accessories, decorative unit, and how they are used. Certain qualities, colors, and textures produce what we understand to be elegant, simple, casual, formal, semi-formal, or informal. In flower show work, then, it is the selected appointments (their quality, style, color, and texture), the plant material, and the design that describe the spirit and formality of the dining table.

BUFFET TABLES

Buffet tables must be engaging, attractive, and functional, and present a picture of irrepressible friendliness. Placement of platters, chafing dishes, etc. should be convenient and easily accessible. Plan your equipment to indicate the type of food and the type of buffet (brunch, luncheon, dinner, tea, supper). Do not clutter your table with too many appointments. On the other hand, be sure not to have them so sparse as to indicate inadequate provision to feed your guests.

In placing your china, platters, casseroles, napkins, and decorative unit, give particular attention to the over-all balance. A large article, such as a platter, tray, chafing dish, salad bowl, or decorative unit, at one end of the table must be balanced by another such large object or group of smaller ones at the other end of the table. If you mentally divide your table as in Chapter 5, you can distribute your appointments either symmetrically or asymmetrically, so that equal visual weight (good balance) is achieved. This is particularly important in buffet settings.

DOILIES

Doilies and mats may be used for all types of settings, ranging from the most formal to the most informal. The quality and color determine where and when they may be used appropriately. However, few flower shows provide exhibitors with beautifully finished tables; therefore, doilies are not generally used (exception: House and Garden Shows). A center runner is not necessary when place mats are used. It is optional, though it is rarely used today, because the exposed wood, marble, glass, or synthetic finishes, such as vinyl plastic, are most attractive. On a narrow table it is far better to omit the center runner for comfort and beauty. If the table has a protective and handsome finish, it is possible to reverse the order and use only a center runner and omit the place mats, or to omit both. This is often done in modern settings.

CANDLES

Candles serve a trifold purpose:

1. They contribute soft light which adds sparkle and romance to the setting.

2. They become part of the vertical design and as such can be used for greater or lesser height, as required. For visual comfort, candle flames should be above or below the eye level of your guests. They should never be the same height as your centerpiece. Lower or higher adds variety and interest to the vertical design.

3. Candles can accent a color theme. The colors you select should be subtle, repeating in some value the color of your table covering or a color note in your china, crystal, or decorative arrangement. The old idea that white or ivory candles are best on every table is no longer accepted. White or ivory candles, not related to one or more of the dominant appointments, colorwise, can upset the total visual ensemble. Use white candles only when and where they are appropriate; use them with a white cloth, or for dramatic contrast on a dark, vibrant cloth, possibly emerald green, shocking pink, or Persian blue, with white appointments. Dark or bright candles are more difficult to use successfully. But in the right setting, for a special occasion, they can create a striking picture. The right color in candles can do much to unify a table.

Candles may be used on dinner tables and tea tables. They are not used, and logically so, for luncheons because there is no need for candlelight during full daylight. There are a few exceptions, such as a wedding breakfast or luncheon where candles, traditional and symbolic, add to the glamour of the occasion. In flower shows, the tips of the candles may be burnt to give your setting a realistic touch, but it is not required.

To prevent candles from burning down too quickly, keep them in the refrigerator several hours before use.

Subtle decorator colors in your candles can be easily achieved if the colors you desire are commercially unavailable. Use soft pastel chalk, rub it lightly on the candles, wipe with a damp cloth, and blend until the color is satisfactory. Try combining several colors for different and charming effects (see Chapter 8).

CANDLESTICKS

Candlesticks may be used singly, in pairs, or in groups, depending upon the size of the table.

CANDELABRA

Candelabra generally require a large table to be in proper scale and proportion. To dramatize their beauty, give them their just and appropriate setting.

Check List for Blue Ribbons

Be sure the table is set correctly and neatly.

Be sure that all appointments are appropriate for the particular course the table is set to display. In other words, if the table is set for dessert, all you need is dessert equipment, and if for the first course or main course, use only the needed proper china, crystal, and the like. Do not mix your appointments. Use napkins of the correct size, folded simply according to their design and size (see Chapter 3).

Preferably the tablecloth should be even on all sides with graceful overhang. *Note:* Cloths with rounded corners are more graceful for oval tables.

Be sure to create good design, both horizontally and vertically. A table that is all flat, on one plane, without the variation of height (in glasses, compotes, candlesticks, bowls, flower arrangements), tends to be uninteresting.

Remember to mix and match. Co-ordinate textures, colors, and designs in your appointments for unity, but avoid overmatching. You can match to monotony, if you are not aware of the problem. Do not forget the note of contrast. This surprise quality does much to add interest and unify the dominant elements. Avoid too much variety by introducing too many styles, colors, and textures, as these can produce an overactive, confused table, and thus destroy its quiet and unity. Blending appointments, old and new, or appointments of different origin, is quite acceptable if their spirit is harmonious, if there is a feeling of belonging together, or if their contrast enhances and unifies the dominant motif. Feature a note of inventiveness in a unique design, in distinguished appointments, or in unpredictable colors, like hot pink with orange, peacock blue with violet and coral. Your knowledge of design and your imagination are the gateways to freer interpretation.

Table Settings for House and Garden Shows

Tables and all floral compositions should be set in direct relationship to the room in style, color, and spirit, in House to House, or House and Garden Shows. In order to achieve the best results, the exhibitor should view the home and dining room before the day of the tour and confer with the hostess, where possible.

HOSTESSES' ETIQUETTE
1. Co-operate with the exhibitor, allow her artistic freedom.
2. Assist where possible.
3. Be open-minded; do not demand the same setup as you usually have. New ideas may come from allowing an exhibitor to express herself in your surroundings, bringing new fashion éclat to your décor—ideas you might happily pay for if you engaged a decorator!

CLASS: "A CONTEMPORARY SETTING WITH CLASSIC TOUCHES" Refectory runners of ecru lace and linen leave the center of the lightwood table bare. Venetian birds and candelabrum, Belgian crystal, and heirloom china complement the arrangement. Talisman roses, mignonette, golden apples, grapes, strawberries, and begonia leaves on marble bases are a sumptuous note for this beautifully correlated and lavish setting. *Arranger: Mrs. Richard Nathan.* (Photo: William Sevecke)

EXHIBITORS' ETIQUETTE

1. Be understanding and co-operative.

2. Try to keep the flavor and spirit of the room by co-ordinating all appointments in color, texture, and spirit (style) in relation to the table and background.

3. Arrange to see the home ahead of time by appointment, at an hour convenient to the hostess. It is best for the committee chairman to arrange a particular day and hour at which time the exhibitor may view the home in which she is exhibiting and talk with her hostess.

4. Co-operate with the hostess in ideas or suggestions wherever possible. If they are in direct opposition to your plans, discuss them ahead of time and explain your ideas diplomatically—with a velvet touch. Too many accessories or small things on the table, buffet, or server detract from the setting. If you meet this problem, request in a very gentle way that some of the lovely things be removed for safety. Too many accessories, no matter how lovely, detract from one another. Therefore, highlighting a few is always more effective.

5. Flat silver is generally used on a table exhibited in a house and garden tour.

6. Remember, you are a guest in the home of another. Be considerate (neat, quiet, and careful) while working.

7. On the day of the tour, arrive at the time designated, not much before or at the last moment.

8. Ask when it will be convenient to remove your things. Do so at that time. Be sure to thank the hostess for her generosity and leave things, as nearly as possible, as you found them.

TO JUDGE OR NOT TO JUDGE

Most house and garden tours or shows are noncompetitive. The purpose is to allow complete freedom of expression, unhampered by a designated schedule or by competition. However, there are some clubs that plan competitive tours because they often serve as their yearly or semiannual flower shows. How to judge House and Garden Shows is discussed in Chapter 14.

Because a flower show or an exhibition hall is a place people pass through rather than linger in, arrangements and settings can be and should be more striking and original than for your home. At home a room is designed for relaxation and entertaining and so your decorative notes should be interesting and appealing, but need not be boldly demanding. A flower show exhibit should be dramatic and exciting. It should be the source of new ideas and artistic floral inspiration. This is the challenge of exhibiting.

Chapter 14

JUDGES AND JUDGING

I tolerate with the utmost latitude the right of others
to differ from me in opinion. THOMAS JEFFERSON

JUDGING can be fun even though it is a sobering and serious business. It will help you, as conscientious as you may be, if you can maintain your perspective and your sense of humor. Accordingly, I am sure this will enable you to see things in their true light—objectively, and to appreciate the beauty, spirit, and dilemmas in the exhibits and in so many situations.

To judge means to evaluate, appreciate, review. It means also to give criticism, to give an opinion, to arrive at a decision, to award a verdict.

The Judge

A good flower show judge is one who is recognized for her work and who is accepted as an authority in her field; one who is modest and able to judge with understanding and without prejudice. It is necessary also for a judge to be able to state her views and opinions clearly and to justify her decision intelligently and unemotionally.

Should the judges ever be uncertain about a minor technicality, they should err on the side of leniency and not penalize the exhibitor. Should they detect a slight flaw or irregularity which does not detract from the over-all beauty of the arrangement or the setting, they should not stress it out of all proportion.

QUALIFICATIONS OF A GOOD JUDGE

There are several qualifications and attributes that make a good judge; some are innate, some acquired. To be a competent judge, a comprehensive knowledge of the subject is necessary. It is generally attained through study and application. In the case of flower arrangements and table settings, the following are essential:

1. A knowledge of the principles of design, their practical use.

2. An understanding of color, technically and artistically.

3. An ability to recognize plant material and its suitability in the individual arrangement.

4. An appreciation of the intent of the exhibitor and a willingness to give due credit for the inspiration behind each arrangement. Being an exhibitor oneself helps one in being tolerant and aware of the problems involved.

5. A complete comprehension of the schedule attained by careful study and analysis *before* starting to judge. Too many times points of importance have been overlooked because the schedule was read too casually.

In addition to the practical and technical knowledge of the subject, there are other qualities that make the difference between a judge and a superior judge. They are sensitivity, insight, understanding, consistency, and logic. Also stability, objectivity, open-mindedness, and kindness. These qualities or the lack of them color the decisions of the judges.

Obviously, personalities, personal likes, or unfortunate personal experiences should not enter or be reflected in making decisions. There is no room for prejudice if one is to be a conscientious, capable judge. Judging should be objective, not subjective.

It is good to be courageous, but not dogmatic. It is important to believe in yourself. If you feel you are right, arrive at your decision after due and thoughtful consideration. Seek to be constructive in your analysis, not just to please. The decision of the judges is final, and the majority always rules. Constructive comments from respected judges encourage exhibitors, particularly those who may not have received recognition. As judges we should strive to grow artistically and become more flexible and liberal. Only then can we ever hope to stimulate and recognize creative work. These, I believe, are the prime qualifications and responsibilities of a good judge.

Process of Judging

Point scoring or point judging is a matter of appraising. If a proper scale of points is established, it is an aid to students or inexperienced judges and of value to experienced judges in case of close competition.

In judging flower arrangements and table settings, there are certain fixed elements and principles which must be considered, plus the intangibles of interpretation, originality, and distinction. Point scoring is an aid to arriving, as near as possible, at a fair and just verdict.

STANDARD SYSTEM OF POINT SCORING

There are several systems of point scoring. However, the one used by most clubs and recommended by the National Council of State Garden Clubs is the Standard System.

THE CHARM OF MONOCHROME The varied textures and forms add interest to this contemporary setting in green. Succulents, aucuba, pepperomia, and ivy are deftly organized in sculptured wood. The striking green and white plate (Bersa by Georg Jensen), green woven straw mat, gold-green napkin, heavy Italian goblet, and celadon candles are harmonious and appropriate modern accents. This easily designed arrangement is effective, inexpensive, and long-lasting. (Functional capsule setting) *Arranger: the author.* (Photo: Richard Knapp)

TIMELESS BEAUTY Vibrant and delicate colors combine to give this setting a special charm. Displayed against an orchid linen-and-silk cloth background, the alabaster compote, bird, and candlesticks reflect a timeless quality. The Pucci-designed plate, sheer crystal goblet, and tall white tapers denote today's elegance. In contrast, the arrangement of grapes, apples, crab apples, pears, and euonymus provides a lusty note. (Exhibition capsule setting) *Arranger: the author.* (Photo: Richard Knapp)

In the Standard System each quality has a perfection mark. Exhibits are measured against those ideals, and the resulting figures of each quality are added to make the score. In this system, only one Blue Ribbon (1st), one Red Ribbon (2nd), and only one Yellow Ribbon (3rd) may be awarded. There may be several white ribbons, Honorable Mentions, if the class is good. If the class is poor, one or more awards may be withheld.

Experienced judges do not point score each arrangement. They first review the show, then appraise the class carefully. Each exhibit is mentally evaluated against perfection (100 per cent). Those which fall far short are eliminated after due consideration, and the remaining exhibits are scored for final decision. In close competition, it is wiser for judges to point score entries vying for the awards.

AWARDS IN THE STANDARD SYSTEM OF SCORING

1st or Blue Ribbon—must score	90 points or more.
2nd or Red Ribbon—must score	85 points or more.
3rd or Yellow Ribbon—must score	75 points or more.
Honorable Mention or White Ribbon—must score	65 points or more.

The Tri-Color Award, the Award of Distinction, and the Award of Creativity are the crowning awards given only to an outstanding exhibit, scoring 95 or over in a large competitive, praiseworthy standard flower show.

Exhibits eligible for:

The Tri-Color Award must be composed of all fresh plant material. Accessories may be used, but their use must be so specified in the schedule.

The Award of Distinction must be composed of all other than fresh plant material.

The Award of Creativity must include some fresh plant material, and creativity (individual expression) should be the outstanding characteristic of the exhibit. (National Council *Handbook for Flower Shows, 1965*)

Scales of points and other specifications for judging Standard Flower shows (District and State shows) can be found in the *Handbook for Flower Shows* and the subsequent *Flower Show School Directives* issued by the National Council of State Garden Clubs.

In judging, some responses are momentary; other reactions are the result of study. If the exhibit survives both favorably, it undoubtedly has merit.

The scales of points for flower show tables, which follow, may also be used for table settings in competitive House and Garden Shows. You need only substitute Suitability to Background Setting for Conformity to Schedule. Other scales of points for compositions in placement shows will be found in the National Council *Handbook for Flower Shows*.

Judging Flower Show Tables

In judging a dining table in a flower show, appraise it first as a unit for its over-all impression: color harmony, beauty of design, and co-ordinated spirit. Then, after study, evaluate it by reviewing in detail the qualities that make a beautiful, well-co-ordinated table.

1. A plan—a pleasing over-all design.
2. Proper scale of all appointments and flower arrangements.
3. Good proportions.
4. Satisfying visual balance.
5. Rhythmic transitions.
6. Related textures.
7. Harmonious use of color.
8. Emphasis through dominance and contrast.
9. Distinction and/or originality.
10. Compatibility of all materials.
11. Functionalism, practical appointments, properly and conveniently placed.
12. Condition of plant material, fastidiousness in linens, etc., and precision in settings.
13. Conformity to schedule, occasion, or interpretation.
14. Over-all unity, harmony, and spirit.

JUDGING THE CENTERPIECE

Now, in judging the centerpiece or decorative composition, consider it as a complete entity, not as previously evaluated in relation to the setting. Judge it first for:

1. Spirit, appropriateness to the schedule requirements.
2. Excellence and faultlessness of design, pleasing silhouette, good proportion, consistent scale relationship, balance and stability, and dominance and contrast.
3. Harmony of color.
4. Originality and/or distinction in plant material, idea, and craftsmanship.
5. Compatability of all materials, plant material, container, and accessories, if incorporated.
6. Condition, freshness, crispness, clarity of the plant material, meticulousness of anything associated with the centerpiece (container, base, accessories, and water, if it is part of the arrangement).

The centerpiece or decorative composition is generally viewed from many angles and so should be finished all around to fulfill this requirement. It need not be the same on each side; in fact, diversity is more interesting.

CLASS: "MERRIE MONTH OF MAY: A SPRING LUNCHEON"   The over-all setting is fresh and charming, the colors are gay and harmonious. All appointments are related in color and agreeable in texture and spirit. The arrangement is in good scale, balance, and proportion; however, real distinction could be achieved if the structural voids had greater diversity. Appointments: coffee and brown straw mats, two-tone green faïence (Nils, Denmark), and green-footed goblets. Plant material: forsythia, ligustrum, jonquils, andromeda, and yellow-green succulents. *Arranger: the author*. (Photo: David L. Steindler)

Point Scoring Flower Show Tables

Scales of points may be adjusted to suit the specific class. The following may serve as a guide:

I. OVER-ALL DESIGN	20%	Balance (visual) proportion, scale of all appointments in relation to each other and to the flower arrangement; appointments practically and correctly placed—rhythm; dominance, and contrast.
II. DISTINCTION AND ORIGINALITY	20%	Superior quality, decidedly different; expert craftsmanship; new idea; use of unusual materials and color harmonies; clever use of the usual; smartness; style.
III. COMPATIBILITY OF ALL MATERIALS	20%	Relationship of textures, color harmonies, over-all unity, with a note of contrast; appropriate and functional accoutrements or lack of them.
IV. PERFECTION OF CENTERPIECE	15%	All principles of good design apply (should be related in color, texture, and/or spirit to over-all setting).
V. CONFORMITY TO SCHEDULE, SUITABILITY TO OCCASION, OR INTERPRETATION	15%	Appropriateness; functionalism; spirit—adherence to theme.
VI. CONDITION—FASTIDIOUSNESS	10%	Plant material, neatness of all appointments; precision and meticulousness.

SUGGESTED SCALES OF POINTS HIGHLIGHTING SPECIAL CATEGORIES

Over-all design	20	20	20
Distinction and originality	20	15	20
Compatibility of all materials	20	15	15
Perfection of centerpiece	15	20	20
Conformity to schedule, suitability to occasion, or interpretation	15	20	15
Condition—fastidiousness	10	10	10
	100	100	100

ART OF GRACIOUS DINING Charming traditional setting well designed in color and spirit. Appointments: gold and green place plates, gold-banded bread-and-butters (Limoges) to match dinner plates, sterling silver candlesticks, handmade ecru lace doilies. The centerpiece of red roses and snow-on-the-mountain is free, yet controlled. The setting rates fairly high on all counts but one—functionalism. Can you detect why? The exhibitor neglected to include napkins, thus penalizing herself and reducing the possibility of a top award. *Arranger: the author.* (Photo: William Allen)

Schedules

Schedules should be imaginative and well written. All classes should revert to the theme. The requirements and restrictions should be limited, but not limiting, stated simply and clearly, with consistency and without contradictions. Clarity eliminates controversy and facilitates judging.

A schedule that is inspiring and flexible stimulates the exhibitor to participate, which, in turn, makes for a large and exciting show. A well-written schedule is both a guide and an aid to both the exhibitor and the judge. For maximum efficiency and understanding, advanced scrutiny is a must.

The exhibitor must be aware of the limitations of the schedule and the potentials and opportunities for imaginative interpretations. So must the judge!

Here are a few suggested themes for schedules and related classes. They are simply written, proposed to inspire and stimulate the exhibitor, thus allowing her and her imagination freedom and latitude, unhampered by too many restrictions.

THEME AND CLASSES

RETURN TO ELEGANCE

Classes

1. The Gracious South

   A contemporary dinner table with a traditional flavor.

2. Tea in a Rose Garden

   A tea table, roses to predominate.

3. Bridal Tea

IMPRESSIONS AND EXPRESSIONS

Classes

1. In the Cool of the Evening

   A table set for terrace dining.

2. Dining Abroad

   A luncheon for two, reminiscent of a foreign land.

DELICATE PORTRAITURE—BRIDAL TEA Depicting a setting sans table, the background-foreground is a white embroidered nylon cloth lined with pale green, with a *bouffant* tulle skirt to the floor. Appointments: lily-of-the-valley china, white linen napkins, silver tea service on a footed silver tray. The delicate arrangement on the Sheffield candelabrum is composed of white roses, Snowdrift chrysanthemums, white snapdragons, and white carnations with variegated miniature ivy. *Arranger: the author*. (Photo: William Allen)

WE WOMEN   PAST—PRESENT—FUTURE

Classes

1. My Business Was My Pleasure.

   A luncheon depicting a business or profession.

2. Fun with the Family.

   A family dinner for a particular occasion (birthday, holiday, etc.).

3. Fashion Futures

   Sophisticated dining, with color emphasis.

The number of place settings and other requirements must be designated either along with the class or in the rules.

Illustration of a Judging Experience

CLASS
A spring table set for breakfast.

DESCRIPTION
Table was set with a gray burlap cloth, pewter plates, pewter mugs, dark gray napkins. A piece of flagstone was used as a container base, on which an arrangement of jonquils and narcissi was built. Stones and moss were accessories.

JUDGE'S COMMENTS
The table was beautifully co-ordinated in color, texture, and design. It had charm and distinction in its organization and restrained presentation. The simple arrangement was well designed and skillfully executed. The whole effect was informal and smart.

The choice of cloth and flagstone, however, was unfortunate for a spring breakfast. The effect though striking was severe and failed to carry the spirit of either spring or breakfast, which should be gay, delicate, fresh, and practical. In the scale of points it would therefore be pointed down in appropriateness and interpretation.

Had this table been entered in a class calling for a terrace or patio luncheon, the results would have been different. In this case there is fine relationship of materials (in color, texture, and spirit). They are indeed appropriate to the theme. This understated but smart interpretation produces a highly distinctive table.

The following scale of points shows you how the same exhibit rates differently, depending upon the class.

ORIENTALE INTIME   Appointments of different origins and cost, compatible in texture, color, and spirit, are combined with finesse to create an Oriental mood. An arrangement in the Oriental manner sets the scene: quince branches and camellias in light red and galax and ivy foliage on an original frosted-glass plaque mounted on a lacquer stand. The Blush china picks up the colors of the arrangement beautifully. For those who cannot manipulate chopsticks, black and gold Far East cutlery is shown. In judging, this attractively co-ordinated table would rate high, but it would not receive full count for fastidiousness because of the lack of precision in the placement of tea cups and glasses. *Arranger: the author.* (Photo: William Allen)

		Spring Breakfast	Terrace Luncheon
Over-all Design	20	19	19
Distinction and/or Originality	20	17	18
Compatibility of materials	20	17	18
Perfection of Centerpiece	15	14	14
Interpretation, Suitability to occasion, Conformity to schedule	15	11	15
Condition-fastidiousness	10	10	10
	100	88	94

The ultimate in the art of table setting for home or flower show requires the ability to interpret your ideas with simplicity and artistry—the ability to bring to your designed setting those intangible, priceless qualities of drama, distinction, originality, and finesse.

Above all, your success will come with technical know-how by combining all to create visual beauty, appropriateness, and functionalism, with good taste.

145

Chapter 15

THE NEW EMPHASIS

I N the not-too-distant past an impressively set table was an integral part of the comfortable, well-ordered home. In general, elaborate and elegant appointments adorned the dining tables. Some were beautiful in design and quality, others just costly and overdone. Their compatibility, scale, and appropriateness to the table or to the style of living were not always apparent because the value of the accoutrements was all important. Though the individual appointments in themselves may have been artistic in design, thought was rarely given to organizing them in scale, color, texture, and spirit.

Tables of the past reflected plenitude rather than selectivity, and frequently ornateness rather than elegant simplicity. Paraphernalia itself seemed most important, and "more rather than less" was always preferred. Often so much equipment was used on the table that the pieces vied with each other for attention.

Simplicity Versus Clutter

The past makes the present meaningful, and beautifully designed and elegant appointments of any era continue to be a joy. But today expensive, elaborate appointments do not necessarily make a truly exciting table setting. It is primarily fresh ideas, new presentations, and an attractive simplicity that distinguish tables of the mid-twentieth century from those of the past.

Study, travel, and rapid communications are bringing distant lands closer. We are becoming familiar with other peoples, their way of life and their contributions to our culture. Their color combinations, fabrics, china, and art objects are no longer strange to us. New paths and procedures in science, industry, and the arts, too, form our tastes and add a new dimension to our creative work. The result has brought about striking changes in all creative media, especially in the decoration of our homes.

The contemporary smart table is frequently as beautiful as the traditional table of the past. Its success stems from selectivity, originality, imagination, and good taste in the combination of appointments.

Modern appointments can be blended successfully with those of the past. It takes just a little thought, understanding, and cultivated taste. Be sure when combining them to emphasize a dominant *style, color scheme, era,* or *idea.* This will give your table a feeling of unity even though you choose diverse appointments from the past or from other lands. Organize your equipment, flower arrangement, and accessories in *color, texture,* and *spirit* to highlight your idea, the theme, or the occasion for the setting. *Keep your table uncluttered;* this will give it a well-groomed and more effective appearance. The well-dressed table, like the well-dressed woman, is beautifully coordinated, strikingly charming, and never overdone.

Remember, today's rule of thumb is: less rather than more.

Space Placement

Space placement creates areas that, by contrast, emphasize the objects they surround.

Never before has the element of space taken on such importance in the art fields—perhaps because we are living in the space age. In the past we created design by the orderly organization of lines and masses in relation to one another. The resultant voids, which contributed to the interest of the design, were unplanned. Today the approach is different. The designer regards space as a design element, knowing that space is as essential to design as are line, form, and color.

In flower arrangement and table setting, as in sculpture and painting, designs that enunciate interesting voids and just the right areas of space, within and around, are most effective. Sculpture, some abstract flower arrangements, and assemblages in particular depend for their success on proper space placement.

Nothing supports or emphasizes the beauty of the elements of your table setting as well as planned space placement. Areas of space should be consciously arranged (1) by allowing adequate room between settings; (2) by not crowding the setting itself with too many appointments for too many courses at once; (3) by grouping appointments and accessories, particularly smaller items, which should be grouped in twos, threes, or fours to give the effect of a single unit; and (4) by avoiding monotony through too even placing of accessories and decorative units—always introduce some variation.

Interestingly planned spaces produce attractive design patterns and relief areas. When appointments are effectively organized and distributed, the resulting space enhances them. An area of space around your decorative composition lends it importance. Space also functions in design; through its contrast to form, color, and pattern it points up the unity and beauty of the setting.

The clever use of space is the hallmark of gracious contemporary dining. A crowded table is neither comfortable, practical, nor pretty. The setting should be designed to put

SUKIYAKI TONIGHT
Serene, restrained, and articulate is the subtle blending of floral centerpiece and appointments to create an Oriental feeling. The graceful figurines repeat in subdued tones the vibrant orange of the showy Oriental poppies. The table covering is a soft jade green. *Arranger: the author.* (Photo: William Allen)

guests at ease; gracious dining is relaxed dining. Remember that even if you do your own serving, do not crowd your table. Teacarts and convertible tables, so popular today, aid in convenient service and keep your table uncluttered.

In a flower show an exhibitor should try to capture this vital quality. Too many or too varied appointments, accessories, or decorative units spotted around can spoil the effect. A cluttered, busy table is disturbing both physically and visually. Good design, correlated appointments, interesting space placement, and creative ideas are the important features of contemporary table settings.

Chapter 16

NEW CATEGORIES IN
TABLE SETTING SECTION

*E*NTHUSIASTIC interest in exhibiting and viewing table settings in flower shows continues steadily to increase—so much so, that many large flower shows now assign a separate section and additional awards especially for the table setting division.

A table setting section of the artistic division of a standard flower show is composed of a number of classes and exhibits designated in the National Council *Handbook for Flower Shows*. If the minimum number of classes designated are included in this section, the garden club or group of garden clubs may apply for a top award (see 1965 National Council *Handbook* and 1966 additions).

There are two categories that may be exhibited in the table setting section: *complete settings* and *capsule settings*. Each category may be further designated as either functional or exhibitional as the schedule requires.

FUNCTIONAL TABLES are *objective, realistic, utilitarian,* and/or *interpretative.* They should:

1. Show correct placement of proper and appropriate appointments, decorative unit, accessories; e.g., velvet, lamé, and chiffon are inappropriate table coverings.

2. Carry the spirit of the occasion, express a theme.

3. Suggest the meal to be served—the course or sometimes the menu, as in a buffet setting.

4. Display artistic over-all design, emphasizing the relationship of practical and artistic elements—correlated in color, texture, and spirit.

Functionalism in table setting is essential, for it shows how food may be served in the most practical and attractive manner. Selection, correlation, and logical placement of

AN AURA OF SPICE   A simple, charming setting is created through restrained and subtle use of muted spice colors. The woven straw mat is of golden mustard and dill, with a curry-colored napkin. The same colors are repeated in the pottery plate and in the arrangement. Yellow day lilies and iris foliage in an allspice-colored pottery container are accented by coral. The candle and Degas head are in shades of cinnamon, clove, and allspice. The crystal goblet is peppery brown. (Functional capsule setting) *Arranger: the author.* (Photo: William Sevecke)

realistic appointments reflect an understanding of functionalism in table setting. So important is functionalism in table setting that all settings are exhibited and judged as "functional" unless the schedule specifies otherwise. However, to avoid confusion it is always best to stipulate in the schedule the type of table desired.

EXHIBITION TABLES are *subjective*, generally *nonutilitarian*, and/or *interpretative*. They must:

1. Reflect a clever combination of equipment (dramatic, different, even impractical) but *must be* attractive.

2. Be well-designed, harmonious in color, texture, and spirit.

Exhibition settings are "for effect only." Practical placement of appointments and logical combinations are not essential, but there must be some relationship to dining.

The exhibition table or setting is a decorative, artistic display, an organized aesthetic presentation. Emphasis is placed on originality, distinction, good design, color coordination, and interesting textural compatibility. It is the clever selection, placement, and association of all material that are important. This type of table need not be entirely functional; the over-all effect must be one of a unified ensemble that may be purely decorative, interpretative, or even subjective (abstract).

DESIGNED FOR TODAY No. 1 Sparkling emerald green and royal blue dominate this setting. On the floor-length blue and green cloth rest a navy blue place plate, a blue and white entrée plate and white soufflé dish, an opaque green goblet with a white lining, a pewter candelabrum, celadon green candles, and an arrangement of various hues of green foliage (pale green scolopendrium and dark green horse chestnut). A muted-red figure accents the arrangement and dramatizes the setting. (Functional capsule setting) *Arranger: the author.* (Photo: William Sevecke)

DESIGNED FOR TODAY No. 2 Although similar appointments are shown, the illogical placement clearly depicts how setting No. 1 has been effectively transformed. This is non-functional and used "for display only." (Exhibition capsule setting) *Arranger: the author.* (Photo: William Sevecke)

Complete table settings usually require service for four or six. The number should be stated in the schedule. Complete table settings have been covered in considerable detail in earlier chapters. Discussed here is the new technique of exhibiting table settings in a flower show in the category known as *capsule settings*.

Capsule Table Settings

A capsule setting is a compact version of a larger or complete table setting. It may be designed in two ways:

1. A section of a larger table, generally displayed on a smaller table. The decora-

GREENSLEEVES   A subtle elegance is at work here. The green-gold table covering is echoed in the Italian pottery plate, chartreuse goblet, and hand-fringed linen napkin. The exquisite forms and colors of the roses and the Japanese dahlia, scolopendrium, and velvet-leaf anthurium frame the matte-textured chartreuse candle. (Functional capsule setting) *Arranger: the author.* (Photo: Richard Knapp)

HARVEST SONG Provincial vitality pulsates from this setting. In striking contrast with the warm tones of the pumpkin-colored background, bittersweet tapers, pyracantha berries, and amber-tinted goblet is the elemental blue and white Arabia pottery. The majolica candelabrum holds a graceful arrangement of pyracantha, quince, apples, sickle pears, crab apples, and little green Italian peppers. The walnut napkin ring enclosing the pumpkin linen napkin resolves the harmony of Harvest Song. (Exhibition capsule setting) *Arranger: the author.* (Photo: Richard Knapp)

tive unit should be in scale and proportion to the larger table (approximately five feet, unless otherwise stated) even though it is shown on the smaller table.

2. Against a specified background with some appointments that suggest dining (plate, napkin, glass, etc. and decorative unit with or without accessories). The space allotted or the size and type of the table must be designated in the schedule.

A table set for one or two and meant for one or two is not a capsule setting; the arrangement, accessories, and appointments must be in proportion to the specified table size.

Capsule settings exhibited on small tables may be either *functional* or *exhibitional.* Capsule settings staged against a background are always exhibitional.

The *functional capsule table* is a small edition of a large table. Table covering, appropriate appointments, and decorative composition are necessary. The setting should be practical and the equipment logical and properly placed for the specific course. One setting is generally shown, though the schedule should specify requirements fully.

The *exhibition capsule table* is shown "for effect only." It may be staged on a small table with or without a background but generally is designed against a background, in an allotted space. Other designated areas may be a niche, a frame, an individual table, one of a series of spaces on a long table, or a section of a large round table.

EXOTICA Striped madras table covering of American Beauty, rose-violet, lavender, blue-green, and gold enhances the motif set by the blond wood-sculpture (Thai). American Beauty candles, blue-green pottery and glassware re-echo the colors of the background. The arrangement of dried bamboo stalks and fishtail palm, orange and violet-red dahlias, red-orange pyracantha, velvet-leaf anthurium, and rex begonia foliage highlights the theme. Unusual placement of napkins creates variety. *Arranger: the author.*

153

GRANADA Striking appointments with a Spanish flavor are beautifully staged on a straw mat: green and brown Aztec stoneware, amber hand-blown tumbler, wrought-iron candlesticks, blue and green beeswax candles, and blue napkin. (Napkin ring is handmade of floral wire taped with black satin ribbon.) Fantail willow, bird of paradise, and cherry laurel are excitingly arranged in a Spanish amber and black pottery container. *Arranger: Mrs. L. J. Weissenberger.* (Photo: Richard Cobb)

Fabric, stained, or painted wood or synthetic material may be used for background where one wishes to simulate a bare table. However, table cloths, mats, or fabrics should be used as the table covering.

Though the combinations of accoutrements and their placement need not be realistic or logical, the presentation must be properly balanced, in good scale, and in proportion to the assigned space. Striking color and textural effects add a novel note. The equipment, too, must be harmonious in texture, color, and design. Obviously, there must be some association to dining tables in the selection of accoutrements, but distinctiveness, creativeness, and beauty of the design are paramount in the setting that serves "for effect only." Traditional and conventional interpretations *can* be expressed in exhibition capsule settings, but they are less than usual.

A capsule setting allows complete freedom in presenting fresh ideas, novel groupings, and new possibilities for table décor. A welcome and useful entry in flower shows, the capsule setting requires *less space, smaller tables, freer presentations, limited equipment,* and *reduced physical effort*. The accent is on distinctive appointments, creative designs, and imaginative combinations. Exhibitors, judges, and the public alike find this a new and challenging contribution to the art of display in table setting and flower arrangement.

Chapter 17

NEW CONCEPTS

*A*n artistic achievement is the subtle marriage of elusive and dynamic qualities. The melding of an original concept with distinguished execution spells success in any art medium—sculpture, painting, flower arrangement, and table décor in both traditional and contemporary expressions. An awareness of these essentials is the first step in creative, artistic thinking.

Some artisans and judges have wandered far in trying to keep abreast with the times. We frequently hear: Do anything different or shocking to attract attention! And many do. This attitude is found, perhaps, among the less informed, the inexperienced and untutored, because "a little knowledge is a dangerous thing."

Being different seems to be the directive of our times. Some exhibitors and judges feel that whatever is different is all important, whether or not the difference has anything vital to impart. But without an idea and fundamental knowledge we are mere copyists, producing nothing more than stilted imitations. For example, many of us were once unthinking slaves to our early technical training, and as a result, our flower arrangements were superficial, neither stimulating nor satisfying. They fell far short of artistic achievement because neither honest ideas nor knowledge of fundamental design was apparent.

Do not misunderstand. I am not belittling new ideas, fresh enthusiasms, or daring experimentation. On the contrary. I feel we must be receptive to untried efforts. But we must be able to differentiate between empty imitation and genuine creative merit.

In any endeavor we must exercise *both* imagination and skill. To follow routine in our everyday or artistic pursuits is to become dull and static, both in spirit and in mind.

Change means progress, but many of us find it difficult to break away from the comfort of sameness and familiarity. People say, "Change isn't necessary; we are happy as we are." But whenever we are objective, unbiased, and receptive, we find change a source of new ideas and satisfaction.

FRESH AND FANCIFUL
This garden-fresh setting finds inspiration in the cranberry and hot pink shades of the hollyhocks, the cocks' combs, the straw placemat, the varicolored printed napkin, and the band of the goblet. The pastel-colored pottery plate subtly re-echoes this impression. The amusing use of cut lily stalks adds a note of distinction to the garden material. (Functional capsule setting) *Arranger: the author.* (Photo: William Sevecke)

As judges and exhibitors, our eyes, minds, and hearts must be alert and sympathetic to excursions into the unfamiliar. Much inspiration may be garnered from a look at the past as well as from adventures into the future. New ideas and expressions are the life's blood of creative work.

I, for one, believe there is much for us to explore. A departure from the usual or traditional, even though it may be unsettling at first, is healthy and stimulating. We need not, however, march blindly with extremes. Difference for the sake of difference is not enough. Bizarre combinations and expressions in themselves rarely produce the distinction, freshness, and dramatic impact we hope for. Conflicting colors and textures, grotesque shapes, weird combinations, and extreme proportions, lacking proper relationship, organization, and continuity of thought, can be distracting and unmeaningful. The ultra extreme expressions used to shock can be successful when the artist reflects an inner emotion and executes it with skill, but they have no place in table settings that must insure peaceful gracious dining.

Things or ideas that are different or unique may have in themselves a quality of distinction and, of course, can be used to great advantage. It is your own keen, sensitive understanding of what these objects and colors will do when combined and how they can be used to translate your ideas that will create the "something new" for which you are

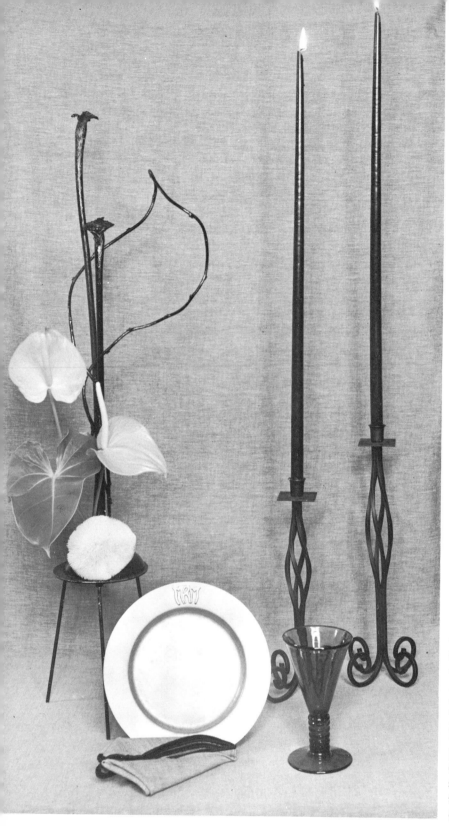

ULTRA SMART Bold contemporary concept, emphasizing dramatic contrast and space. Subtle salt and pepper denim cloth is foil for black wrought-iron candlesticks, very tall candles, tripod, wisteria branch, and schefflera stalks. Handmade pewter plate and heavy green Italian goblet are a pleasing blend. Red anthurium, cut philodendron, and white spiral coral accent and unify the design. (Exhibition capsule setting) *Arranger: the author.* (Photo: William Sevecke)

striving. The sincere artist has the individuality and the awareness to select, limit, and organize objects and colors expertly.

We must allow ourselves to be receptive, to be stimulated by the wonder and variety of the world if we want to be attuned to new ways of thinking.

A truly creative idea is the beginning. The successful translation of it into visual expression (a flower arrangement, table setting, painting, etc.) is achieved through knowledge and experience, the handmaidens of creative interpretation and fine craftsmanship. A knowledge of the principles of design and their application can develop your original concept into a distinguished accomplishment, be it traditional, avant-garde, or completely subjective (abstract).

Whatever you do in creative work today, have something to say. Say it simply and directly and let it be an expression of your own. Do not be a copyist of either the traditional or the avant-garde schools. Do not try to imitate exponents of other media literally, without regard to the purpose and demands of your own. If you do, then you will be no different than we were in the early days of flower arranging, when we slavishly copied the Japanese. Our art, of necessity, soon reached a plateau, and we stood still for several years.

Since the early 1900s there have been explosive changes in the arts. Flower arrangement was slow to be affected, but at last it is animated and we now see exciting changes.

To say that all things of the past would be unacceptable to us in contemporary table setting would mean we were blind to much of our inspiration. We do not discard the Old Masters because present-day artists express themselves in an entirely different manner. Even though we burst with new ideas and new equipment, we do not reject the lovely accoutrements of the past in favor of only the sleek and colorful appointments now available. Fine china, delicate and exquisite table coverings, and elegantly wrought silver always have a place, even in our most modern table settings. How, when, and where we use these appointments of the past is the test of their appropriateness.

Shops today offer an abundant variety of possibilities for table settings with co-ordinated linen, china, and crystal. Such ensembles can be a tremendous help if selected carefully and not used to excess. Obviously, every detail need not match.

Preplanned table equipment, much like a TV dinner or packaged food, is convenient but sometimes impersonal. It cries for a personal touch—maybe an antique box to hold your flowers or candlesticks from a foreign land. Your creative ideas will make it *your* individual setting.

The modern concept of table setting calls for a smart simplicity, simplicity in equipment and restraint in its use. A note of re-echoing elegance serves, through contrast, to accent the simple lines, vital color harmonies, and interesting space areas we love to use today. Table settings have taken on the fashion of our times. They are gayer, fresher, more stimulating in the use of color, patterns, and texture. I firmly believe that the artist in contemporary table setting *should free her creative spirit and let it sway, but balance it*. The appreciation and application of new concepts initiate "the fresh look" of unforced charm, communicating smartness and giving pleasure always.

QUESTIONS AND ANSWERS

A reasonable probability is the only certainty.

E. W. HOWE

1. WHAT MAKES A PRIZE-WINNING TABLE SETTING?

An inspiration, skill to execute it, distinction, an original quality, functionalism, and attention to detail.

2. HOW SHOULD DINING TABLES BE JUDGED?

They should be judged as they are to be used. For a seated meal, view table from a seated position; for a buffet, view it from a standing position. A free-standing table should be viewed from any or all sides, unless the schedule states otherwise. Many buffet tables are designed to be judged only from the front and sides.

3. HOW SHOULD ONE JUDGE TABLES IF NO SCALE OF POINTS IS SUGGESTED?

In judging tables without a given scale of points, judges should choose one suggested in the *Handbook for Flower Shows,* or they may formulate an appropriate scale of points. When doing this, it is necessary to remember that the over-all effect is paramount. No part is greater or more important than the whole. Try to give each quality its just consideration. Do not emphasize or dwell unduly on any one facet, good or poor, thus giving it more importance than it deserves. Keep in mind always the schedule requirements. Does it fulfill them? As an artistic achievement, how does it rate? As a table setting, is it functional?

4. CAN ONE USE DOILIES FOR A BUFFET TABLE?

No. Doilies indicate individual place settings. If used, they would cause spottiness, making it very difficult to achieve an organized, well-balanced buffet table.

5. MAY A BUFFET TABLE BE SET FOR ANY COURSE?

Yes. It must, however, present the proper and complete appointments to indicate the specific course, such as first course, main course, dessert, or tea.

6. WHAT ARE THE MINIMUM NUMBER OF APPOINTMENTS REQUIRED FOR A BUFFET TABLE?

In addition to plates, glasses, and flower arrangement, there should be serving dishes indicating the type of menu. Perhaps a platter to hold the roast, a casserole, vegetable dishes and/or a salad bowl. Bread trays, salts, and peppers may be added if they

160

contribute to the design. They are not essential in flower show settings, if the other equipment is sufficiently descriptive. Candlesticks, candelabras, compotes, tea service, or other appropriate accessories may also be incorporated to enhance your table.

7. ARE WATER GLASSES GENERALLY USED ON A BUFFET TABLE?
They are not generally used on a luncheon or dinner buffet table, but should you plan the kind of buffet in which you would be serving a cold drink with the main course or dessert, the pitcher or punch bowl should accompany the glasses.

8. WHEN A CLASS ASKS FOR A "HOLIDAY TABLE" SHOULD THERE NOT BE SOME EVIDENCE OF THE HOLIDAY OTHER THAN THE WRITTEN DESCRIPTION?
Emphatically yes, through the color, decorative composition, and accessories. Often the appointments indicate the holiday, such as turkey plates for Thanksgiving. Other appointments and accessories can also convey the theme: appropriate favors, place cards, candles, plant material, and special tablecloths (Christmas, Valentine's Day).

9. HOW DO YOU DETERMINE THE NUMBER OF POINTS TO BE DEDUCTED IF MECHANICS ARE OBVIOUS? FROM WHICH CATEGORY SHOULD THEY BE DEDUCTED?
Mechanics are essential equipment. If they show slightly but do not detract from the design or all-over beauty of the arrangement, one or possibly two points may be deducted from the category listed as Distinction, because distinction refers to execution or expert craftsmanship. However, if the mechanics are quite obvious and destroy or detract from the beauty and design, the exhibitor must be penalized accordingly. If the fault is very glaring, points may be deducted from either or both Distinction and Design. However, the exhibit should not be penalized twice for the same fault, but the penalty should be distributed in number and category where it belongs.

10. IS A NAPKIN NECESSARY WHEN SETTING A TABLE FOR THE DESSERT COURSE AT A FLOWER SHOW?
It is essential that the schedule clearly state exactly what is required. For a dessert course at the end of a dinner you would not replace a fresh napkin at each setting. However, there are many occasions when only dessert is served—at a garden club meeting, before or after bridge in the afternoon or evening. If a table is set for such a social function, a napkin is in order, even if only for the dessert course. It is difficult to ascertain in a flower show whether previous courses have been served. Therefore, it would seem logical, when a setting for a dessert course is requested, that a napkin would be required to complete the setting, unless the schedule states otherwise.

11. IS FOOD EVER ACTUALLY SERVED ON SILVER OR GOLD PLATES, OR ARE THEY ONLY USED AS SERVICE PLATES?
Yes, silver and gold dinner plates are quite correct for strictly formal services. (Care

must be taken not to serve any acid foods on them, for example, hollandaise sauce, etc.) They were used extensively in England and on the Continent. Those who have them can and do use them. They are in good taste, if all else is in keeping.

12. MAY PLACE MATS BE USED FOR A FORMAL DINNER?
Yes. If they are delicate in color and exquisite in quality.

13. MAY SERVICE PLATES BE USED AS DINNER PLATES?
The large service plate that we use is typically American. It was made in France especially for American consumption, and it is large for a dinner plate. However, the smaller continental service or place plate can be used as a dinner plate. The large not too ornate service plate is, nevertheless, sometimes used for buffet service.

14. MAY EVERGREENS BE USED IN AN ELEGANT PORCELAIN OR CRYSTAL CONTAINER?
Yes. Some glossy broad-leaved evergreens are compatible and smart, such as euonymus, ligustrum, mahonia, Ilex crenata and convexia and Pieris japonica. In the southern climes you will find camellia, pittosporum, cherry laurel, Burfordii holly, and magnolia, to mention but a few.

15. IS IT POSSIBLE TO USE TWO ARRANGEMENTS ON A BUFFET TABLE?
Yes, providing they are in proper scale to the table. The arrangements may or may not be identical, but they should balance and complement each other.

16. WHY DO WE SHOW CAPSULE SETTINGS IN A FLOWER SHOW?
(1) They serve as a source of new ideas. (2) They emphasize (a) the need for proper scale, proportion, and balance within an allotted space; (b) the relationship of color and textural harmony. (3) They allow for table-setting displays where space is limited. (4) They attract exhibitors who enjoy doing tables but who are reluctant to try full-scale tables. (5) They require fewer appointments and accessories and thus demand less physical effort in packing and transporting equipment and less time in setting up. (6) They provide simple, attractive, novel displays in the table setting section. (7) They offer an opportunity to use new equipment.

17. IS IT NECESSARY TO JUDGE A TABLE IN A FLOWER SHOW FROM A SEATED POSITION?
No. Since all exhibits at a flower show are viewed while standing, the table should be set, viewed, and judged from that position. However, at home for a seated dinner, one should examine the arrangement from a seated position, as the guest would, except in the case of a buffet table.

18. MUST GLASSES BE PLACED ON THE TABLE MATS FOR A FORMAL OR SEMIFORMAL FLOWER SHOW TABLE?
It is optional. The size of the mat determines this. If the mat is adequate in size, it will accommodate the glass. If the mat is small, the glass may be placed either on a small companion doily or on the table.

QUESTIONS AND ANSWERS

19. WHEN A CAPSULE SETTING IS PLACED BEFORE A SCREEN WITH WINGS SHOULD ONE PUT ANY OF THE TABLECLOTH ON THE WINGS OR DISREGARD THE WINGS AND JUST PUT THE CLOTH ON THE BACK OF THE SCREEN?

It is preferable to use only the back of the screen. However, some clever exhibitor may achieve an artistic effect by including the wings, though it is more difficult.

20. MUST A TABLE BE SET IN THE PROPER WAY WITH EVERYTHING IN PLACE OR MAY APPOINTMENTS (PLATE AND/OR CUP AND SAUCER, GLASS, NAPKIN, ETC.) BE PUT ANYWHERE ON THE TABLE WITHOUT REGARD TO LOGICAL PLACEMENT, AS LONG AS BALANCE IS MAINTAINED?

It depends on whether it is a functional or exhibition capsule setting. A functional table must be set logically and employ realistic appointments. An exhibition capsule table may have appointments placed without regard to logic or service, as long as the setting is well-designed, attractive, and balanced.

21. IN AN EXHIBITION CAPSULE SETTING, IF ONE USES A TABLECLOTH ON THE BACK OF A SCREEN AND DOWN OVER THE TABLE, MUST THE PLATE BE ON A PLATE RACK OR MAY IT BE FLAT ON THE TABLE?

For an exhibition capsule setting the plate is usually on a plate rack or stand, not flat on the table because it enhances the over-all effect.

22. SHOULD THE TABLECLOTH (BACKGROUND) HANG OVER THE FRONT EDGE OF THE TABLE OR STOP AT THE TABLE EDGE?

For the best effect the tablecloth should hang gracefully over the edge. If the show committee decides for some reason that the cloth should stop at the edge of the table, exhibitors and judges must be advised. In either case all the exhibits in the class should be staged the same.

23. WHEN A CARD TABLE IS USED FOR A CAPSULE SETTING SHOULD THE TABLE BE SET THE SAME AS WE SET A LARGER TABLE—WITH ONE PLACE SETTING WITHOUT SILVER BUT EVERYTHING ELSE IN THE PROPER PLACE?

How a table is set depends upon the schedule. It should state whether a functional or exhibition capsule setting is called for. Service for one is generally shown.

24. WOULD YOU SUGGEST THAT THE NUMBER OF APPOINTMENTS IN A CAPSULE SETTING BE LIMITED? SOME EXHIBITORS HAVE USED BOTH DINNER AND SALAD PLATES, GLASS, CUP AND SAUCER, NAPKIN, DECORATIVE UNIT, AND CANDLE.

The over-all design within the allotted space and its effectiveness are most important. A crowded setting is unattractive; clutter minimizes the beauty and distinction of a setting. The schedule may limit appointments if the committee so chooses. But whether it does or does not, the exhibit is judged for its good design (scale, proportion, balance, etc.) in relation to the given space and to the other schedule requirements.

25. SHOULD THE SCHEDULE SPECIFY WHETHER THE SETTING IS TO BE FORMAL, INFORMAL, BREAKFAST, BUFFET, ETC. AND STATE THE SPECIFIC ITEMS TO BE INCLUDED?

The schedule may request any style of setting. It is not always advisable to require specific items. Leave something to the imagination of the exhibitor. However, the schedule should state minimum requirements allowing freedom, particularly in the interpretive classes.

INDEX